Signature in the Schools Volume 1

My Vacation in Paris
Salat
Civil Wars
Aftershock
Shakespeare, Will

Joe Calarco

A Samuel French Acting Edition

SAMUELFRENCH.COM
SAMUELFRENCH-LONDON.CO.UK

Copyright © 2015 by Joe Calarco
All Rights Reserved

SIGNATURE IN THE SCHOOLS VOLUME 1 (including *MY VACATION IN PARIS, SALAT, CIVIL WARS, AFTERSHOCK,* and *SHAKESPEARE, WILL*) is fully protected under the copyright laws of the United States of America, the British Commonwealth, including Canada, and all other countries of the Copyright Union. All rights, including professional and amateur stage productions, recitation, lecturing, public reading, motion picture, radio broadcasting, television and the rights of translation into foreign languages are strictly reserved.

ISBN 978-0-573-70462-8

www.SamuelFrench.com
www.SamuelFrench-London.co.uk

For Production Enquiries

United States and Canada
Info@SamuelFrench.com
1-866-598-8449

United Kingdom and Europe
Plays@SamuelFrench-London.co.uk
020-7255-4302

Each title is subject to availability from Samuel French, depending upon country of performance. Please be aware that *SIGNATURE IN THE SCHOOLS VOLUME 1* (including *MY VACATION IN PARIS, SALAT, CIVIL WARS, AFTERSHOCK,* and *SHAKESPEARE, WILL*) may not be licensed by Samuel French in your territory. Professional and amateur producers should contact the nearest Samuel French office or licensing partner to verify availability.

CAUTION: Professional and amateur producers are hereby warned that *SIGNATURE IN THE SCHOOLS VOLUME 1* (including *MY VACATION IN PARIS, SALAT, CIVIL WARS, AFTERSHOCK,* and *SHAKESPEARE, WILL)* is subject to a licensing fee. Publication of this play(s) does not imply availability for performance. Both amateurs and professionals considering a production are strongly advised to apply to Samuel French before starting rehearsals, advertising, or booking a theatre. A licensing fee must be paid whether the title(s) is presented for charity or gain and whether or not admission is charged. Professional/Stock licensing fees are quoted upon application to Samuel French.

No one shall make any changes in this title(s) for the purpose of production. No part of this book may be reproduced, stored in a retrieval system, or transmitted in any form, by any means, now known or yet to be invented, including mechanical, electronic, photocopying, recording, videotaping, or otherwise, without the prior written permission of the publisher. No one shall upload this title(s), or part of this title(s), to any social media websites.

For all enquiries regarding motion picture, television, and other media rights, please contact Samuel French.

MUSIC USE NOTE

Licensees are solely responsible for obtaining formal written permission from copyright owners to use copyrighted music in the performance of this play and are strongly cautioned to do so. If no such permission is obtained by the licensee, then the licensee must use only original music that the licensee owns and controls. Licensees are solely responsible and liable for all music clearances and shall indemnify the copyright owners of the play(s) and their licensing agent, Samuel French, against any costs, expenses, losses and liabilities arising from the use of music by licensees. Please contact the appropriate music licensing authority in your territory for the rights to any incidental music.

IMPORTANT BILLING AND CREDIT REQUIREMENTS

If you have obtained performance rights to this title, please refer to your licensing agreement for important billing and credit requirements.

TABLE OF CONTENTS

Introduction from the Author 7
MY VACATION IN PARIS 9
SALAT..51
CIVIL WARS..93
AFTERSHOCK.......................................145
SHAKESPEARE, WILL 193

INTRODUCTION

I started writing for the Signature in the Schools program ten years ago under the tutelage of the late, great, Marcia Gardner, and I continue to under current Education Director David Zobell. The innovative program, started in 1995 by Marcia and playwright Norman Allen, has had a profound impact on the thousands of student actors who have gone through the program. When Marcia first asked me to write for the program I was unfamiliar with it, and I wasn't sure what I was signing up for, but when she said to me, "I want you to write a piece about the French Revolution in which Sally Hemings, one of Thomas Jefferson's slaves and mother to at least six of his children, is one of the main characters. She was with Jefferson in Paris right before the Revolution broke out. She could have stayed in France and been a free woman. The question I want you to answer in the play is, 'Why did she go back to America with him?' And the play can't be longer than 65 minutes." I knew immediately that I was about to be involved in something very exciting. This was challenging subject matter, and Marcia was adamant that the play not "talk down" to its audience. Writing these plays has stretched me as a writer. Many of the "hot button" subjects we've tackled – the wars in Iraq and Afghanistan, PTSD, the Arab Spring, immigration, Hurricane Katrina, the Holocaust, cyber bullying – I don't think I would have necessarily chosen to write about on my own, but writing them has totally expanded what I want to write about. It's dared me to, and made me want to, write about the politics of our time and how young people interact with the world around them. Over the years the young actors who have performed these plays continually say how exciting it is for them to tackle characters their own age who are dealing with real issues. Over half of the plays include a young character dealing with the wars in Iraq or Afghanistan. By the time I wrote my first play for the program America was engaged in both wars. By the time I wrote my tenth play for the program I realized that no one in the young cast consciously knew of a time when the country they lived in wasn't involved in one or both of the conflicts. Seeing young actors tackle these plays every year has been so inspiring. Often at talkbacks after a performance someone in the audience will ask the cast what they learned from the experience, and they usually mean, "What did you learn about theater?" But almost always the students respond talking about what they learned about the world around them. Working on these plays broadened their world view. Writing them has certainly broadened mine.

– Joe Calarco

For Marcia Murdock Gardner

My Vacation in Paris

MY VACATION IN PARIS was commissioned and produced in 2006 by Signature Theatre in Arlington, Virginia (Eric Schaeffer, Artistic Director, Maggie Boland, Managing Director) for their Signature in the Schools program (Marcia Gardner, Education Director). It was directed by Marcia Gardner, with scenic design by Rich Weinard, costume design by Melanie Dale, lighting design by Ronnie Gunderson; and sound design by Tony Angelini. The cast was as follows:

SALLY HEMINGS	Kristin James
MARTHA JEFFERSON	Laura Downes
MARIA JEFFERSON	Maggie Harrington
JAMES HEMINGS	Ben Truong
OLYMPE DE GOUGES	Hope Lambert
PIERRE AUBREY	Erik Lenderman
SOPHIE	Maria Wilson
CITIZENS	Amanda Donahoo, Brian Eberly, Kevin Trudel

CHARACTERS

SALLY HEMINGS – 16. African American. Slave of Thomas Jefferson. Very light skinned. A dreamer.

MARTHA JEFFERSON – 17. Daughter of Thomas Jefferson. Smart. Contained. A good hostess.

MARIA JEFFERSON – 11. Daughter of Thomas Jefferson. Precocious. Vivacious. An optimist.

JAMES HEMINGS – 19. African American. Brother of Sally Hemings. Chef of Thomas Jefferson. Loyal. Fiercely devoted to his sister.

OLYMPE DE GOUGES – 41. A ferocious advocate for women's rights and a supporter of the aristocracy. A "bohemian."

PIERRE AUBREY – 23. Olympe's son. A French revolutionary. A leader of the rebellion. Passionate. Speaks his mind.

SOPHIE – 20. Haitian. Servant of Olympe de Gouges. Contained. Well educated.

CITIZENS – A minimum of two men and one woman.

SETTING

Paris, 1789.

PRELUDE

(Paris, the summer of 1789.)

*(We hear music of the French court. Lights rise on an ottoman center stage. On it sits **LOUIS XVI** and **MARIE ANTOINETTE**. **MARIE** has a fan covering her face, and a plate with a large pastry sits on her lap. A group of **FRENCH CITIZENS** huddles together staring at them, some using opera glasses perhaps.)*

*(Lights rise on **SALLY HEMINGS**. She faces straight out to the audience.)*

SALLY. Dear Thena. Well, we still here in Paris, and I'm telling you little sister, there's no more thrilling place on God's green earth. Such things as you never did think to see back in Virginia.

> *(**MARIE** lowers the fan to reveal her face. The **CROWD** sighs and rhythmically claps its approval.)*

Even after two years here, every day something I never knew there was, just happens right in front of me, jumping outta nowhere.

> *(**MARIE** takes the pastry from the plate and feeds it to **LOUIS**. He takes a bite. The **CROWD** again sighs and rhythmically claps its approval.)*

Somethin' bright and beautiful that bursts out from around some corner you didn't even know was there.

> *(**LOUIS** and **MARIE** stand up and begin to do a French waltz. The **CROWD** sighs and claps rhythmically again. A man in the crowd [**PIERRE**] starts to stomp his foot rhythmically.)*

There's always something – something ready to wake you up, like from a real deep sleep, making you see things different. But it ain't always a pretty thing, what goes on here. It can be something scary that makes my insides twist up tight.

> *(Another person joins in the stomping as **PIERRE** jumps onto the ottoman and reads from a piece of paper. The **KING** and **QUEEN** continue their dance throughout.)*

PIERRE. The representatives of the French people organized as a National Assembly, believing that the ignorance, neglect, or contempt of the rights of man are the sole cause of public calamities and of the corruption of governments, have determined to set forth in a solemn declaration the natural, unalienable, and sacred rights of man!

> *(More and more of the **CROWD** begins stamping their feet until it is a loud, powerful, steady, rhythm. This sound is augmented with the recorded sound of glass smashing, fire burning, and angry shouting. All these sounds mix with the court music that is still playing.)*

SALLY. But it's living. There's living going on here. A rushing, exciting, kinda thing. Like when we run down the big hill out past the workmen's house and we can't stop ourselves from falling and laughing. That's how I feel here. Like I'm rushing faster and faster and I ain't sure where I'm going but it feels like I can't stop myself from going there. It makes me wanna – ...Well, I got some things running 'round in my head. Some new things I'm thinking.

There's a new dream I'm dreaming.

> *(All of the recorded sounds become cacophonous ending with the sound of someone screaming. Blackout.)*

(Paris. Early September, 1789. In the darkness we hear the hustle and bustle of the streets of Paris. We hear a large crowd chanting in the distance.)

CROWD. *(voice over)* Vive la liberté! Vive la liberté! Vive la liberté! Vive la liberté!

(The distant chanting continues as lights rise on a luxurious, ornate, sitting room. This can be, and maybe should be, represented by a singular divan or ottoman. There are also several packed trunks in the room. Clearly the occupants are getting ready for a long trip. **SALLY** *runs in with a small satchel. She runs to one of the trunks, drops her satchel, and opens the trunk and rummages through it. She gathers some clothes and shoves the clothes into the satchel. She continues to rummage through the trunk looking for more clothes.* **JAMES HEMINGS** *appears in the doorway. He sees what his sister is doing and whispers to her frantically.)*

JAMES. Sally, no.

SALLY. You don't need to be here.

JAMES. This ain't the right time.

SALLY. There ain't never gonna to be a right time. Today's as good as any is ever gonna be.

*(****JAMES**** rushes into the room to try to stop her.)*

JAMES. They're coming.

(She stops packing.)

SALLY. What?

JAMES. They're back from the dressmaker early.

(He moves to unpack the satchel and put her clothes back in the trunk.)

SALLY. No...

JAMES. Please, Sally, we gotta hurry.

> (**SALLY** *grabs the clothes from* **JAMES** *and shoves them back into the satchel.*)

SALLY. No! No! No! No! I can't stay here!

> (*They are both a bit shocked by her violence.*)

I've made my choice... Please. Please tell me you understand.

> (*We hear the laughter of two young women from offstage.*)

MARIA. (*offstage*) Sally! Sally?! Viens vite! [*Sally! Sally?! Come quickly!*]

MARTHA. (*offstage*) Polly, ne cours pas s'il te plait! Grimpe les marches une a la fois sinon tu trébucheras. [*Polly, please don't run! Take the stairs one at a time. You'll trip and fall.*]

> (**JAMES** *quickly stashes the satchel behind one of the packing trunks.*)

MARIA. (*offstage*) Sally ma chère, viens voir! [*Sally dearest, come and see!*]

MARTHA. (*offstage*) Polly, stop all this shouting. The whole of Paris can hear you.

> (**MARIA JEFFERSON**, *called "Polly," runs in carrying a dress box. She is a vivacious eleven-year-old. She drops the box and runs to* **SALLY** *and embraces her.* **JAMES** *backs off.*)

MARIA. Sally, wait until you see. (*calling off*) Patsy, hurry! (*to* **SALLY**) You've never seen anything so beautiful. People will faint from looking at us.

> (**MARTHA JEFFERSON**, *known as "Patsy," enters with two dress boxes. She is a refined girl of 17, clearly the "grownup."*)

MARTHA. Polly, that's enough.

(JAMES hurries over to her and takes the dress boxes from her and places them on the divan. MARTHA smiles at him and he exits.)

I would think after nearly two years in Paris that some sense of refinement would have taken hold. My sister isn't the student you are.

MARIA. Sally, tell her how we chatter away in French all day, every day.

MARTHA. No. Show me. Sally, speak to my little sister. Let's see how her skills have grown.

(MARIA turns and addresses the audience.)

MARIA. I didn't want to come to Paris. Back in America – back home – I'm everyone's favorite. Why even here in Paris there are nothing but smiles when I enter a room. All but my sister. I begged father not to make me join them here. If he hadn't agreed to let Sally come with me, I would have kicked and screamed 'til it was decided I didn't have to go. As it was, I begged and pleaded with him, "Please. I don't want to come. Patsy will do nothing but lord over me." If it weren't for Sally, I couldn't bear Paris, even for all the chocolate and the toffee and the dancing puppets in the streets.

(Lights change and we are back in the scene. MARIA turns back to MARTHA.)

You know that I can speak the language well enough. Why just now with the dressmaker, I spoke only French, and he said I did beautifully.

MARTHA. Yes, but a dressmaker in the center of Paris is not the King of France. You'll be tossed from Versailles like a beggar tonight if you're not careful. But you, Sally, will glitter and shine, like a jewel.

(She opens one of the dress boxes and takes out a beautiful but simple blue gown and holds it up to SALLY.)

Perfect.

MARIA. Wait.

>   (**MARIA** *grabs and opens one of the other boxes and takes out a glittering white gown and hands it to* **MARTHA**.)

Sally, hold your gown up to you and Patsy you take this. And now…

>   (*She runs to the third box and takes out a glittering red gown and holds it up to herself.*)

Stand next to one another.

>   (*She grabs each and arranges them in a row next to each other so the gown colors are in the correct order to represent what would one day soon become the French flag. In this configuration the simplicity and plainness of Sally's gown is highlighted next to the extravagance of the other two gowns.*)

It was Patsy's idea.

MARTHA. We need a proper entrance.

MARTHA. Tell us what you think.

>   (**SALLY** *answers in French.*)

SALLY. Merci les filles. C'est très charmant. Elles sont toutes magnifiques. *[Thank you both. It's lovely. They're all beautiful.]*

>   (*She meticulously takes her gown and lays it out over one of the trunks. Throughout the following she takes the two other gowns and hangs them up; also, so the image of French rebellion is present at all times.*)

MARTHA. I hate to think of leaving, and the days are flying by.

>   (*As* **MARIA** *takes her gloves off she remembers the calling card she has slipped in the wristband of her glove.*)

MARIA. Patsy, we nearly forgot.

>   (*She hands the card to* **MARTHA**.)

MARTHA. Oh yes. Father wouldn't approve.

MARIA. Father has guests all the time.

MARTHA. Yes, but a young girl doesn't make such overtures to strangers on the street.

MARIA. He approached us.

MARTHA. Yes, but –

MARIA. We don't have time to argue this Patsy.

(She runs to the doorway and calls.)

James!

MARTHA. Maria Jefferson! Please.

(She grabs a bell and rings it.)

You astonish me.

*(**JAMES** enters and bows his head.)*

JAMES. Yes. Miss Martha.

MARTHA. Miss Maria has forgotten all sense of decorum and invited two absolute strangers over for the afternoon. Could you fix up something simple to serve in the dining room? There's too much clutter in here.

MARIA. Oh Patsy, they'll understand, and this room is much more suited for conversation. I'm just bursting to meet her, and the minute she tastes James' food, she won't want to open her mouth except to sample more, and we won't hear a word from her. Sally, this morning we heard from at least three or four people that your brother has become the most talked about cook in Paris. He could have any position he wanted. And to think he's all ours.

JAMES. When might they be arriving Miss Martha?

MARTHA. Oh any moment I imagine.

MARIA. Sally, we met the most charming man as we left the dressmaker.

*(She runs to **MARTHA** and grabs the card back and takes it to show **SALLY**.)*

And handsome too.

MARTHA. Polly.

MARIA. There's no wrong in saying so. He's the son of Olympe De Gouges. Have you heard of her? She's a wild, sort of revolutionary eccentric. A writer. All of Paris talks about her and her freethinking politics. She's quite scandalous. And I hear, she takes lovers.

MARTHA. Sister, we do not talk of such things.

(**MARIA** *gives* **MARTHA** *a look.*)

MARIA. Her son stopped us on the street and introduced himself. He said his mother had been anxious to meet us for ever so long and once she heard we were leaving Paris she couldn't hesitate any longer. He was on his way to the house to make his introduction when a friend of his pointed us out on the street. "Fortunately met!" he cried, and we all laughed as if we were lifelong friends.

MARTHA. I didn't laugh. As you grow taller, so do your tales.

MARIA. *(ignoring her sister)* We quickly invited them to join us for the afternoon. He went to collect his mother and we will soon meet this fascinating creature.

JAMES. "Any moment," you say Miss?

MARTHA. Oh yes James, I'm sorry. I know it doesn't leave you much time but you always seem to manage.

JAMES. Why don't I serve some refreshments, here in the sitting room first? That gives you time to greet your guests. Then you can move on into the dining room.

MARTHA. You're a marvel dear James. What will we ever do without you?

(**JAMES** *bows his head and leaves.*)

MARIA. Do you think we have time to freshen up Patsy?

MARTHA. We'll hurry.

(**SALLY** *begins to follow* **MARIA** *out.* **MARTHA** *stops her.*)

No, Sally. If you help her, she'll start chatting about our morning, and our guests will age from the waiting.

We'll manage on our own. You stay here and greet our guests if they arrive early.

> (**MARTHA** *and* **MARIA** *leave.* **SALLY** *is left alone. She goes over and touches the plainer blue gown made for her. She touches* **MARIA***'s elaborate red gown. She holds it up against her. Distant music is heard as if in* **SALLY***'s head. She curtsies as if bowing before a suitor. She turns the other direction and bows to another imaginary suitor. She turns a third time to another. And then rises as if to dance with him. She begins waltzing slowly with the dress held up to her. As* **SALLY** *gets lost in her fantasy she waltzes bigger and bigger until she is dancing around the room.* **JAMES** *enters.)*

JAMES. Don't do this.

> *(Surprised,* **SALLY** *stops suddenly and quickly hangs the dress back up.)*

SALLY. You shouldn't be here. You got work to do. They'll be here any moment now.

JAMES. And you shouldn't be dreaming about something that's gonna lead you nowhere. You can't do a thing like this in your condition.

SALLY. It's just having a baby James. Women do it all the time.

JAMES. Yeah, but most don't run off to hide in some strange country.

SALLY. I'm not hiding.

JAMES. I'm telling you, think about what this is gonna do to you, and your baby.

SALLY. I've made my decision. I don't wanna discuss it no more.

JAMES. It's not only your decision to make. You're a selfish girl. You'll be the ruin of us all.

SALLY. You've got no right to talk about this. You've got your freedom. He's promised it to you. You've got skills he's taught you, and now you only have to train someone else to run his kitchen and you'll be free. You're gonna leave Virginia a free man and leave the rest of us chained to that house. Why shouldn't I want more?

JAMES. You think he's gonna keep his promise to me if you're gone in the morning? What's life gonna be like for any of the Hemings back at Monticello if you run away? We're blessed Sally. We're the house servants of Thomas Jefferson. Where's your loyalty?

SALLY. To who? To him?

JAMES. To your family! *(Realizing his outburst, he whispers.)* If you run, it won't go so well for the rest of us.

(a bell rings)

MARIA. *(offstage)* Oh no!

MARTHA. *(offstage)* Polly, stay calm.

MARIA. *(offstage)* I just need a few more minutes.

MARTHA *(offstage)* Sally, can you greet them and bring them up to the sitting room?

SALLY. *(calling off)* Yes Ma'am.

*(She starts to exit. **JAMES** grabs hold of her by the arm.)*

JAMES. I'm begging you, don't do this.

*(**SALLY** pulls away and exits. **JAMES** exits also.)*

*(**MARTHA** enters and faces the doorway, ready to greet her guests. A moment later, **MARIA** runs in frantically. **MARTHA** quickly fixes the collar of **MARIA**'s dress. Just as **MARIA** turns to face the doorway **PIERRE AUBREY** enters. He is a handsome, striking young man of 23. He holds himself well and has a natural charisma. He is a leader. He begins to bow in introduction but, his mother, **OLYMPE DE GOUGES**, age 41, enters brazenly from behind him, her arm outstretched. She is what we would define as bohemian. She is wrapped in some sort of shawl or cape. She "takes*

up a lot of space." She has a fierce, focused, yet warm energy. Her servant **SOPHIE** *follows behind.* **SOPHIE** *is black, simply dressed, and contained. She has a quill pen, paper, a lap sized writing board, and an inkwell with her.* **SALLY** *remains behind standing in the doorway.)*

OLYMPE. It is pleasure. Yes, pleasure. The total pleasure.

PIERRE. May I introduce –

OLYMPE. – Olympe De Gouges –

PIERRE. – My mother.

OLYMPE. Yes.

PIERRE.	**OLYMPE.**
And I, of course, am –	And this, of course, is –

PIERRE. Pierre Aubrey.

OLYMPE. My son.

PIERRE. Yes. But we've already had the pleasure.

MARTHA. Well… I am Martha Jefferson, and this is my sister Maria.

*(***MARIA*** curtsies.)*

MARIA. A pleasure.

PIERRE. Please accept my apologies for my mother's –

MARTHA. Oh no –

OLYMPE. You don't have to –

MARTHA. No –

PIERRE. She can be –

OLYMPE. Pierre –

MARTHA. Truly –

PIERRE. – eccentric.

OLYMPE. I do bring the embarrassment to my son.

PIERRE. That isn't true.

MARIA. I see no reason for embarrassment.

OLYMPE. Some do take the offense from – how do you call it? – my casual ways.

MARTHA. Oh, no…

OLYMPE. I do not believe in standing on the ceremony. Such niceties lead to the miscommunication. I say do away with all these barriers. We must venture head first into the knowing of one another. It is the only way.

MARTHA. Forgive me, it's just we're not accustomed to such –

MARIA. Patsy, please –

OLYMPE. What is this?

MARTHA. Pardon?

OLYMPE. This word Patsy. What do you mean by this?

MARTHA. It's a pet name.

OLYMPE. Oh, how sweet. *(trying it out)* Patsy. Patsy? Patsy!

MARTHA. It's a name used only by those closest to me.

OLYMPE. Well, we are to be close. I can feel this. We must be as sisters in fact, for we are sisters. Our sex can no longer afford this – this ripping from each other. We must look into the eyes of one another and say up, out into the air, to the world, "We are one!"

PIERRE. Mother.

OLYMPE. I will accept no refusal. And you in turn must call me Olympe.

MARTHA. Oh, I couldn't.

OLYMPE. You must. I insist.

MARTHA. I… I – umm – …

(MARIA looks at her imploringly.)

You may call me Patsy.

OLYMPE. Oh splendid.

MARTHA. But you must allow me my formality and let me address you as Madame.

OLYMPE. Agreed. Let us join the hands on it.

(She holds out her hand for a handshake. MARTHA stares at it then extends her hand. OLYMPE takes it and gives her a vigorous handshake. MARIA runs up, grabs OLYMPE's hand from MARTHA and vigorously shakes it.)

MARIA. You may call me Polly instead of Maria. All my friends and family call me Polly.

MARTHA. Maria!

OLYMPE. Polly.

PIERRE. Mother!

OLYMPE. I must offer the forgiveness for my son ladies. He sees the handshake as a province reserved only for the men. A gesture of business and politics not suited to the female of the species. If it were up to my son, we would only clasp fingers lightly or gently brush each other cheeks with our lips so that we should not dirty our precious womanly skin.

(She looks at her son. After a pause she laughs.)

PIERRE. My mother teases me so. And while I am not as typical as my mother would have you believe, I do bow to the customs of gentlemanly decorum, so you must let me address you as Miss Jefferson and you as Miss Maria.

*(**MARTHA** and **MARIA** curtsy to him.)*

MARTHA. Madame, your son is a gentleman.

OLYMPE. He is nothing if not chivalrous. And now I must ask of you one more favor.

MARTHA. Anything I can grant is yours.

OLYMPE. As you know I am a writer and sometimes I feel the stirring – the explosion – on the inside – the – the inspiration – it is the same, no? Yes. The inspiration from the discussions I engage in day to day that I have found it helpful to have my conversations notated. Now I would not quote you in any way in a published document unless you had granted the permission. It is more for me to look back on the exchanges in hopes of capturing the inspiration once again.

MARTHA. Oh my.

MARIA. Fascinating.

OLYMPE. I usually do not practice the custom on the first meeting with someone. I would not ask for such a breaking of this custom now but for the fact that I have so wanted to meet you and I know that you are leaving us soon and there is no guarantee we will be able to engage in such discourse again.

MARTHA. I cannot deny the request. Sister?

MARIA. How exciting!

> (**OLYMPE** *nods to* **SOPHIE** *who approaches her.*)

I tend to speak quickly when excited. Please don't hesitate to ask me to slow down.

OLYMPE. Sophie is excellent at dictation. She will have no trouble.

MARTHA. Oh.

PIERRE. It is not from laziness or cruelty that she has Sophie do this.

MARTHA. Of course not.

OLYMPE. I cannot read or write.

> (*awkward pause*)

MARIA. Oh my.

OLYMPE. I hold no pride in the fact of it. But I *am* proud I educated my son and that I have educated my mind to appreciate the large thoughts, both others and my own.

> (**SOPHIE** *sits in a chair behind* **OLYMPE** *and writes pretty continuously. From time to time* **OLYMPE** *may glance at her to make sure she is notating something of particular note.*)
>
> (**PIERRE** *notices the gowns.*)

PIERRE. You are caught up in our revolutionary fervor I see.

MARTHA. Pardon?

PIERRE. Your gowns. The colors of the revolution.

MARTHA. Oh yes. *(realizing)* Oh yes! Oh my.

OLYMPE. Is something the matter?

MARTHA. Yes, actually. You see we're to go to Versailles this evening. To watch the King and Queen dine.

MARIA. Isn't it exciting?

PIERRE. It is a strange spectacle I think, inviting people to come line up and parade by, one by one, to watch the royal couple fatten themselves while peasants starve in the streets.

(Lights rise dimly on a crowd of **CITIZENS.***)*

MARIA. Oh.

MARTHA. It is merely sport.

PIERRE. Yes. Well, you must wear them then. It will have quite the effect on the King and his wife.

MARTHA. But not quite the effect I had imagined. Oh my. You see I wanted us to make an entrance.

OLYMPE. That you will do.

PIERRE. It's quite brilliant really.

MARTHA. Well, no, you see I hadn't thought of the colors in that manner. This is what happens when vanity takes hold.

OLYMPE. Even in the brief moments I have known you I cannot imagine that vanity is of the possibility in you. Tell us of your predicament and we will give what counsel we can.

MARTHA. You know of the Queen's latest fancy?

PIERRE. Which one? There are so many.

OLYMPE. *(scolding)* **PIERRE.** *(to* **MARTHA***)* Go on my dear.

(Lights change and the **CROWD OF FRENCH CITIZENS** *turns and addresses the audience. Court music is heard in the distance.)*

MALE CITIZEN #1. All of Parisian society rushes to keep up with the Queen's changing fashions.

FEMALE CITIZEN. One week the court is filled with lavender and emerald gowns to remind her majesty of Spring, the next scalloped white and silver lace to bathe the palace in Winter.

MALE CITIZEN #2. Last month it was "the death of Autumn."

MALE CITIZEN #1. Not Autumn itself mind you.

MALE CITIZEN #2. No, no, no.

FEMALE CITIZEN. No vibrant yellows or reds.

MALE CITIZEN #1. But brown.

MALE CITIZEN #2. Dull, ugly, rotting leaves like brown.

FEMALE CITIZEN. Brown upon brown.

MALE CITIZEN #1. Every dressmaker in the city was frantic to find new shades of brown to die their lace.

FEMALE CITIZEN. Brown lace. Can you imagine?

MALE CITIZEN #2. It did not go so well.

MALE CITIZEN #1. It is said that when her majesty saw everyone assembled she could not hide her disgust.

MALE CITIZEN #2. She ordered everyone away, screaming, screaming that such ugliness should never hinder her sight again.

FEMALE CITIZEN. She burned her own gown that very night.

MALE CITIZEN #1. Brown is now banished from Versailles.

FEMALE CITIZEN. So now the Queen must have only vibrant color.

MALE CITIZEN #2. This week she flew open the calendar and said, "Bring on all the seasons. Let us see the whole year in one night."

(The court music cuts out. Lights back to normal as the scene continues. The **CITIZENS** *look on.)*

MARTHA. So I thought we would bring her the colors of our American seasons. Red for our trees in Fall, blue for the Summer river waters, and white for our Winter snow-covered fields. And I thought, "Oh how clever I am. Yes, we'll represent the seasons as the Queen demands, but when we stand together we'll also bear a resemblance to the American flag. We will not go unnoticed." Vanity. You see? It was all for vanity.

PIERRE. Our Queen takes to vanity.

MARTHA. But I didn't think of the fact that they are also the colors of your rebellion. We'll be ordered away from her presence and return to Virginia humiliated.

OLYMPE. I think she will applaud your courage.

MARTHA. Pardon?

OLYMPE. She is a powerful woman. She respects other women who do not shy away from having the opinion.

PIERRE. Unless they contradict her own.

MARIA. I must say Madame, you're not what I expected.

MARTHA. Polly! *(to* **OLYMPE***)* Do forgive her.

OLYMPE. Oh no. We are all the friends here. My dear Polly, what did you expect?

MARIA. Well, from what we've heard of your politics I didn't think you would be a supporter of Marie Antoinette.

OLYMPE. We all have our whims. You may not agree with her decrees, but you must honor her for the accomplishment. Yes her tastes may seem frivolous but she herself is not. Non, non, non. She is no bauble on the arm of our King. She is his equal, if not more, in all things. She is great with the influence and the power.

MARTHA. Some say she has too much of both.

PIERRE. Precisely.

MARTHA. It's said she can bend the ear of the King in any way she chooses.

OLYMPE. I would rather a woman bend his ear than a man – some advisor grasping for power. Our queen can be of great help to us.

PIERRE. My mother believes in the monarchy.

MARIA. Really?

OLYMPE. Once again Pierre, you give the wrong idea of me. Do I believe that the monarchy is repressive, antiquated- the system that should not exist? Yes. Do I believe that this system should be ripped down right now? No. We cannot be ready for this. *(to* **MARTHA** *and* **MARIA***)* My son and the others like him, they shout for freedom. They promise this to the people, and the people, they listen. But they do not see what will come. It cannot be imagined...the terror.

(A mob turns and each addresses the audience.)

MALE CITIZEN #1. My wife and I. We believe in the rebellion. From the very beginning. "Freedom for all!" But as the weeks, months go by, the anger does not know where to go, in what direction to lead itself. Bigger and bigger it grows, until they are running, through the streets, attacking all they think have...more than they do. I stood in the doorway of my shop and begged, "I am one of you. Freedom for all!" But they do not see me. They see scarves. Winter is coming. That is what they know. So they do not see me, or my wife, or our baby – our home. They see warm wool. It is no time – I cannot even count the minutes it takes – it is that fast. They take it all. And then, they set the fire. So we stand in the street and watch all we have worked for, burn. When it was done, there was no sound. I could not speak. The baby did not cry even. This silence went on and on. And I thought, "Maybe we are the only ones left. Maybe they have burned down the entire world."

MALE CITIZEN #2. He was a tyrant. This aristocrat. He did not know what a day is like for us. I march. I chant, "The time has come!" People must pay for what they have done. I think, "We get him. He will be tried. And we will listen and we will pass judgment." So we arrive at his home. But there is no listening. Only shouting and screaming, and just as he opens his mouth to answer to the crowd, a sound comes out, like he has to take air in big and quick. And then I see it. Through his chest. The spike. The man behind him holding the end of it, pushes it deeper and deeper. A cheer goes up. I look down into the crowd and they swarm on him, like insects on a dead bird. And a woman, she stands over him, pulls his head back and takes a knife to his throat. She cuts and cuts until his head is in her hand. I go with them through the streets. I cannot stop myself. It is like I am being pulled by a hand I cannot see. And soon I am running and screaming with the head in my hand. The things we do that day – the things that *I* do that day. But they must be done. The alternative – the starving, the prison for no reason, no trial, no law to protect us, watching our children die from hunger with no hope to feed them- these things can no longer be. We had to stand up. So there is terror, yes, but... There is a price for freedom.

FEMALE CITIZEN. I did not think of the rebellion. I have a child. My husband is dead. I cannot think of rebellion. I hear the laughing of my son in the street. Then there is the roaring and the screaming. Smashing glass. And voices. Many voices. The roar comes with no warning. And then it is over. They have moved on. The mob. The normal sounds of the street, they are turned back on. Except I do not hear my son laughing. I go to run out the door. But it is blocked. I pound and pound and tear away at the hinges with my hands til they bleed. The door, it comes off. And there, there is my child pinned – ...crushed into the doorway by a runaway cart. It has been some time, but I still do not know what to make of this. It has not broken into the heart yet. But I think, "Is this what they have been fighting for? Is this what comes of revolution? Do we all have the right then to demand our own justice?" Well, where is my justice? Who do I kill now for my justice?

(Lights change. We are back in the scene.)

OLYMPE. We must be ready for it, or the chaos will come. Laws. Pass the laws. Gain the rights for all within the monarchy first, then perhaps the revolution can come.

MARIA. It's unfortunate we hadn't met earlier. We could have arranged for you to meet our father.

OLYMPE. It is not Thomas Jefferson I most wanted to meet but his daughters.

MARTHA. It's kind of you to say so.

PIERRE. I however have had the privilege of meeting your father. I remember the first time I met him, I thought,

"I am shaking the hand that wrote the Declaration of Independence."

MARIA. How splendid. Do tell us where you met him.

PIERRE. Why in this very house. Your father has been of great help to some of us here with our political causes.

MARTHA. Yes, so we hear.

MARIA. We both have been off at the convent for our schooling, and when he took us out of school saying we must prepare for the journey home I shouted, "Hurray," thinking we would at last spend time with him in Paris. But he is gone nearly every day.

MARTHA. Polly, let's not bore our guests with our tiny troubles. We understand that he must attend the debates of the National Assembly at Versailles, and we are proud of it.

MARIA. I don't understand why he must go every day.

MARTHA. Polly!

PIERRE. You must understand your father's knowledge is invaluable. Coming from a country which has successfully passed through a similar struggle that we as Frenchman now face, his acquaintance is eagerly sought, and his opinions carry with them great authority. Why at times it feels like he is the oracle at Delphi and we are all supplicants aching for some seed of knowledge that will be the key to break us from our shackles.

OLYMPE. Be careful Pierre, Sophie's hand will cramp before tea is served.

MARTHA. Well… Father does indeed love France. He seems to think the debates are going quite well and that soon all Frenchmen will have the rights they deserve. A constitution. It will be glorious for France.

(JAMES enters with refreshments.)

MARIA. Vive la liberté!

PIERRE. We shall see.

(awkward pause)

MARTHA. Ah, yes! Thank you James.

(During the following **JAMES** *will serve tea and pastries to the guests.)*

I take it you don't agree with my father's prediction sir?

PIERRE. Let me simply say I find some of his recommendations...mild.

OLYMPE. My son sees all things in the universe as merely planets that were placed here simply to revolve around his blazing sun.

PIERRE. *(laugh)* Sharpen your quill Sophie. My mother enjoys nothing more than a lecture based on my shortcomings.

OLYMPE. All that I am saying Pierre is that Mr. Jefferson's stay in France has nothing to do with you or your dreams of revolution. His duties are confined to the subject of America's commercial relations with France. He has been kind enough and interested enough to give his counsel concerning your cause. You cannot have expected him to join you in storming the Bastille.

MARIA. Oh my, were you there?

OLYMPE. Of course he was there. My son prefers to jump over diplomacy and leap straight into chaos.

MARIA. Father came to the convent to tell us what had happened, but you were there. What was it like?

MARTHA. Polly.

MARIA. Oh Patsy, here's an eyewitness to history. Father would urge us to learn what we can from him.

OLYMPE. Yes Pierre tell them. Tell them the story of rioting in the streets for no reason.

(The **FRENCH MOB** *appears.)*

PIERRE. No reason?!

MARTHA. Pardon me sir, but I don't understand the need for such violence, for the brutality of that day when the Assembly was working on drafting a document that would grant you all you desired.

MARIA. The Declaration of the Rights of Man and of the Citizen.

OLYMPE. Curious title.

(The **MOB** *addresses the audience. [When a / occurs it is a designation that the next line should start. This sequence has much overlapping.])*

THE MOB. The National Assembly recognizes and proclaims, in the presence and under the auspices of the Supreme Being, the following rights of man and of the citizen:

CITIZEN #1. Article number one –

CITIZEN #2. Men are born and remain free and equal in rights

CITIZEN #3. These rights are liberty, / property, security, and resistance to oppression.

CITIZEN #1. Article number nine –

CITIZEN #2. As all persons are held innocent until they shall have been declared / guilty,

CITIZEN #3. Article number eleven –

CITIZEN #1. Every citizen may, speak, write, and print / with freedom.

CITIZEN #2. This declaration –

CITIZENS #3 & #1. – being constantly before all the members of the Social body –

CITIZENS #3, #1, & #2. – shall remind them continually of their rights and duties!

(Lights down on the **MOB.** *The scene continues.)*

MARTHA. A glorious document. Based on America's own Declaration of Independence.

PIERRE. Precisely. I must say I find it curious that the daughter of the man who wrote that document would not understand our plight.

MARTHA. I understand the plight but not the violence. A constitution is what you need, not violent revolution.

OLYMPE. Precisely. But there is no patience in men.

PIERRE. *(laugh)* Do you think the adoption of the Declaration would ever have happened if we had not stormed the Bastille? We were the cause. That prison was the symbol of our treacherous monarchy. We scaled it. We breached it, declaring freedom for all.

OLYMPE. For all? Do you know dear Patsy that there were only seven prisoners inside? Four forgers, two lunatics, and one dangerous pervert.

PIERRE. Oh mother, you of all people should not be so literal. It was a symbol.

OLYMPE. For which ninety-eight of you died.

PIERRE. It was worth their sacrifice.

OLYMPE. Ask that of their families.

(pause as they realize they are guests in someone's home)

We do go on.

PIERRE. Do forgive us.

MARTHA. Oh no –

MARIA. We enjoy debate.

OLYMPE. And I am enjoying these pastries. They're delicious.

MARTHA. Aren't they? Dear James.

PIERRE. Yes. James.

*(He walks over to **JAMES**.)*

All of Paris knows of your culinary talents. You must stay on with us here. Proclaim your freedom.

OLYMPE. Pierre!

PIERRE. What Mother? You are as against slavery as I am. Miss Maria here says the Jeffersons enjoy debate. Why should we not broach the subject?

OLYMPE. Because we are guests in this house! We did not come here to argue slavery with the daughters of the great Thomas Jefferson.

PIERRE. Oh didn't we?

MARTHA. My father is a good man. An honorable man. He believes in liberty for all.

PIERRE. And yet he owns slaves.

(OLYMPE stands to leave.)

OLYMPE. We are leaving.

MARTHA. No. My sister is right. We were brought up on discussion, on not fearing debate.

(OLYMPE sits.)

Mr. Aubrey you seek my father's counsel. You appear to respect his views. And yet clearly you condemn his actions.

PIERRE. I do not mean any disrespect. But I do not understand. We, all Frenchmen, look to your revolution with awe. It inspires us. Except for that one sin. How can you have fought for freedom while keeping so many in chains?

MARTHA. My father tried to amend the Declaration and abolish slavery as France has done but Congress wouldn't allow it.

PIERRE. Perhaps he did not try hard enough.

OLYMPE. Pierre!

MARTHA. These things must be done in steps. And my father prays that the members of our human family may, in the time prescribed by the Father of us all, find themselves securely established in the enjoyments of life, liberty, and happiness.

PIERRE. How can he own members of that "human family" then?

MARTHA. At Monticello, we – we do not engage in – ... That is to say we don't use – ... There are brutal tactics, I know, barbaric methods that some – ... *We* do not do such things!

*(All are surprised by this uncharacteristic outburst from **MARTHA**.)*

I – ...I apologize. I – I –

(**MARIA** *goes to her sister and takes her hand.*)

MARIA. James, tell them. *(to* **PIERRE***)* My father is going to free him. We are not what you think.

(**PIERRE** *goes to* **JAMES** *and holds out his hand for a handshake.*)

PIERRE. Congratulations.

(**JAMES** *looks at it and simply nods his head.*)

JAMES. Miss Martha I ought to go and check and make sure they're doing all right in the kitchen.

PIERRE. May I ask you a question James?

(**JAMES** *looks to* **MARTHA**.)

MARTHA. You may stay James. Lunch can wait.

JAMES. Yes Miss.

PIERRE. Have you thought of staying in Paris James? You are greatly respected here.

JAMES. I gotta go set things right back at Monticello first. Train someone to run the kitchen.

PIERRE. Ah. I see.

JAMES. Then I'm a free man.

PIERRE. Do you have a wife, children?

JAMES. No sir.

PIERRE. Will you try to find your family? We hear of so many families being ripped from each other, bought and sold.

JAMES. All my family's at Monticello.

MARTHA. All our house servants are Hemings.

MARIA. Sally here. She's James' sister.

PIERRE. Miss Sally how do you feel about your brother leaving?

SALLY. Sir?

PIERRE. Once he gains his freedom, it may be a very long time before you see him again.

OLYMPE. Pierre, this has gone on quite long en –

(**JAMES** *speaks up, interrupting, quite unlike him in public. His speech is for* **SALLY**.)

JAMES. I'm coming back sir. Back to visit and such. I wouldn't leave her. I know what it would do to me if she went up and left with no sign of coming back. It'd just about kill me, it would. So I wouldn't do that. Not to my Sally.

MARIA. Of course not James.

(**JAMES** *turns and addresses the audience.*)

JAMES. But that's exactly what I went up and did. I taught my brother Peter all I learned. I left Monticello. Mr. Jefferson, he asked me back. When he became President, he asked me back to be head chef at the White House. Imagine that. James Hemings chef of the White House. I didn't go. I figured that's what I did here in France. I was his chef. I was paid. I couldn't go back and be that same thing to him no more. Even though I wouldn't be his slave by the law of it, every time I'd look at him I just knew I'd *feel* like his slave. So I didn't go. I was free. But really, I didn't know how to *be* free. Mr. Jefferson he taught me how to cook, how to speak French, how to write in my own hand even, lots a things. But not how to live as a free man. It's not as easy as you'd think. Not in America with all that'd people been taught. Not even up North. I took to drink. I died in Philadelphia. I was only 36 years old. The day I left Monticello was the last time I set eyes on my sister. Never did get myself a wife to give me children. So that's all I left behind – that I didn't go back when he asked me, that I said, "No. I'm free." Not much to leave behind I guess, but that's all there is. All except what I left at Monticello: an inventory of the kitchen. Some old French recipes. All written in my own hand.

(**MARTHA** *turns and addresses the audience.*)

MARTHA. "Dearest father, I'm writing to you because I so rarely see you at home these days and I feel the need to put my words down in a more formal manner. We had guests today. Fascinating guests and… Something has happened father. I – I have seen – …Do you recall when we would take our walks around Monticello at dusk just as the sun was setting? It's your favorite time of day. You would say 'Look Patsy. Look how the fading light blurs all things: the trees, the grass, the sun-streaked clouds.' And I would start to squint because I'd start to lose the stark outlines of the surrounding objects as the sun sank lower and lower on the horizon. And you would say, 'Don't look too hard Patsy. You must enjoy the view as it is: all things blended together. Don't work too hard to see all the details clearly. This is God's gift to us, this time of day, with its softer view.' Well father, sitting in my room tonight I thought back on our view and it's as if my memory is altered. I don't remember the wash of trees and grass and clouds as clearly. But I do suddenly remember the hard outline of the workmen's house and the silhouette of James through the kitchen window sweating over a stove and of Sally's tired bent over back as she bandaged Peter's blistered feet and of Bett and Nance holding Critty as she cried in their arms. The list is long- the list of slaves – of – of human beings that we own. I see them clearly now. They are no longer blurred with the beauty of the trees and of the grass and of the clouds. They are clear to me now. And the beauty fades. Your dearest Patsy."

(Lights back to normal.)

JAMES. *(to* **MARTHA***)* I really ought to be out in the kitchen Ma'am if you want lunch on time.

MARTHA. Yes James. Yes of course.

> **(JAMES** *leaves. The air is thick with silence.* **MARTHA** *looks off after* **JAMES. MARIA** *moves to* **SALLY** *and touches her hand.* **SALLY** *pulls it away.)*

PIERRE. It is a grand thing your father has done freeing that man.

OLYMPE. You are a careless man.

PIERRE. Pardon?

OLYMPE. You are so blinded with your cause that you cannot see the pain of human suffering right in front of your eyes. You blast through here as if you were torching the Bastille all over again.

PIERRE. You wrote a play condemning slavery, and yet you chastise me for forcing an argument on the subject. What happened to your battle cry?

OLYMPE. Exactly. Freedom *for all.*

PIERRE. I don't understand.

OLYMPE. You see my dear Patsy, my darling Polly. My son can sit here and bellow about America having committed the sin of not granting all of its Citizens full rights. And yet he fails to notice that we here in France have committed the same sin.

PIERRE. We do not have slavery here.

OLYMPE. No, but under your new perfect vision of France not all Citizens will have equal rights.

PIERRE. *(laughs)* Mother you've gone mad. Of course they will.

OLYMPE. You see dear ladies he does not see what is right in front of him.

PIERRE. Pardon?

OLYMPE. Look around you dear son. You are the only man in the room. And when your glorious revolution comes to pass you will be the only one of us here who will have full and equal rights under the law.

*(long pause as **PIERRE** can say nothing)*

Oh Sophie, jot this down. Pierre Aubrey, son of Olympe de Gouge is left speechless by his mother.

PIERRE. We should go mother.

OLYMPE. You have been invited to lunch. It would be rude to leave.

PIERRE. We are going mother.

OLYMPE. We are not. In fact, Patsy, Polly, I have started some new writing that I would like to have your opinion on. Sophie? Follow along and let me know if I miss anything. But I will not. The words will never leave my brain.

> (**SOPHIE** *leafs through some pages and pulls out a sheet and follows along with* **OLYMPE** *as she speaks...*)

PIERRE. Mother, what are you doing?

OLYMPE. I call this The Rights of Women. "Man, are you capable of being just? It is a woman who poses the question; you will not deprive her of that right at least. Tell me, what gives you sovereign empire to oppress my sex?"

PIERRE. Mother –

OLYMPE. "– Go back to animals, consult the elements, study plants –"

PIERRE. Mother, stop it.

OLYMPE. "– search, probe, and distinguish, if you can, the sexes in the administration of nature. Everywhere you will find them mingled; –"

PIERRE. You cannot – ...Stop, you cannot –

OLYMPE. "– everywhere they cooperate in harmonious togetherness Man alone –"

PIERRE. This is obscene!

OLYMPE. "– wants to command as a despot a sex which is in full possession of its intellectual faculties!"

> (**PIERRE** *finally runs to* **SOPHIE**, *grabs the page from her, and crumples it up.*)

PIERRE. What were you thinking?

OLYMPE. Oh I have only just begun. That is just the introduction. The rest is to be called "The Declaration of the Rights of *Woman* and the *Female* Citizen."

> (*Lights rise on the* **FRENCH MOB**. *A* **FEMALE CITIZEN** *addresses the audience while* **OLYMPE** *speaks to her son.*)

OLYMPE & FEMALE CITIZEN. Article number one: Woman is born free and lives equal to man in her rights.

(*Lights down on the* **MOB**.)

PIERRE. You will not.

OLYMPE. I will.

PIERRE. They will not stand for it, the leaders of the rebellion.

OLYMPE. But they will hear it. And one day it will come to pass and *all* the people of France will indeed be free.

PIERRE. Do you see the puppet shows in the streets mother? They place Marie Antoinette at a tiny guillotine and the crowd laughs and laughs as her head falls into a basket. That will come to pass for the real queen. She has too many ideas and does too many things that too many people do not agree with. And when the power shifts, they will kill her for it. Make sure you are on the right side when the shift happens or I fear you will face the same fate.

OLYMPE. I am no Queen.

PIERRE. But you are a woman with large ideas. France is not ready for such things. I am not ready for such things.

OLYMPE. Will you be holding the basket for my head then?

PIERRE. No. But I will not try to stop the blade from falling either.

(*Pause. He turns to face* **MARTHA** *and* **MARIA**. **PIERRE** *bows*.)

Ladies. Thank you for a lovely afternoon and I do so hope you enjoy the rest of your stay in our fair city. Bon voyage.

(**PIERRE** *gives one last look to his mother and he leaves*.)

(*pause*)

OLYMPE. My, my, I could not write a play with so much drama if I tried.

(**JAMES** *enters*.)

JAMES. *(to* **MARTHA***)* Miss Martha the lunch is ready.

MARTHA. Thank you James. *(to* **OLYMPE***)* Are you sure you –

OLYMPE. Of course. Sophie, you stay in here. I will not need you. *(She takes* **MARTHA** *by the arm)* For from now on we will only chat of the weather and of gossip and of the fashion of the day.

> *(She and* **MARTHA** *exit, followed by* **MARIA**. **SALLY** *and* **SOPHIE** *are left alone. There is an awkward pause. Finally* **SALLY** *smiles and busies herself.* **SOPHIE** *just sits and watches her. Finally,* **SOPHIE** *speaks.)*

SOPHIE. You are a foolish girl.

SALLY. Pardon me?

SOPHIE. I see.

SALLY. Pardon?

SOPHIE. Your plan.

SALLY. I'm sorry, I don't understand.

SOPHIE. No, you don't. You must return to America. You cannot stay here.

SALLY. I must apologize. There seems to be been some misunderstanding. We're all leaving in just a few weeks time.

> *(***SOPHIE** *stands and picks up* **SALLY***'s satchel that was hidden behind one of the trunks.)*

SOPHIE. I think we understand each other quite well.

> *(Pause.* **SALLY** *cannot decide whether to continue to lie or to beseech* **SOPHIE** *as an ally. Finally,* **SALLY** *goes to her.)*

SALLY. I beg you not to tell.

SOPHIE. Do not beg in front of me.

SALLY. I'll ask you then.

> *(pause)*

SOPHIE. I will not tell.

SALLY. I – I've been planning for months and months, ever since it was announced we were going back to Virginia.

SOPHIE. You do not belong here. You cannot stay.

SALLY. But I can belong. I speak the language, and... I – ...I can pass.

SOPHIE. And what will you become here, a former slave woman living free in France?

SALLY. I will *be* free. That's enough.

SOPHIE. Is it? You will be like me. Though your beauty and your skin will doom you to worse.

SALLY. There's no worse than what I have now.

SOPHIE. Your hope will make it worse. You hope for better. I read and write for an illiterate white woman with grand ideas. She speaks of freedom and equality, and yet I cannot marry or have children while I am in her employment. That is not freedom to me.

SALLY. You got the right to choose to leave.

SOPHIE. There is no work. So yes I can choose. I can choose starvation and poverty in the streets, scrounging for bread.

SALLY. But you're an educated, black, free woman in France. There has to be more for someone like you.

SOPHIE. *(laughs)* Someone like me? In Haiti my family had money and power, a plantation, and yes, slaves.

*(**SALLY** is speechless.)*

When I was born, they moved us to France pretending that they still had power, and spending like they would always have money. In Haiti their power and wealth came from owning slaves. There was no power for them here, so they poured what money was left into me. I was sent to study. I learned to read, to write, to speak French, English, German. They thought it would give me something- a better life. I was "an educated black woman" with no means. My family's money was all gone. My parents gave up. I had to come to Paris to make money. But I couldn't find work. My skills are useless. I can read Shakespeare, I can debate, but I can't sew or weave or bake.

SALLY. But listen to you. You've got ideas. You've got big things to say.

SOPHIE. They do not listen to my employer and she is white. How would they ever listen to me? So, one has to survive. I took this job. And now I take down speeches that I could be – *should be* – writing myself.

SALLY. You still got better than most. I don't see a reason for complaint.

SOPHIE. It's not complaint. It's the simple truth. Some black slaves in your own country would bristle at *your* selfish ingratitude.

SALLY. What for?

SOPHIE. I see no evidence of the lash on your skin. You and your brother hold coveted positions in one of the most revered homes in America. The daughters of Thomas Jefferson treat you as a sister. You are better off than many slaves in your country and yet you wish to leave. You hope for better. I urge you to define better for yourself in a realistic manner. We are women. No matter the shade of our skin. There are rights we do not have. And we will not have them in our lifetime.

SALLY. But Madame, she says that we will have –

SOPHIE. The financial support of her lovers allows her to not have to worry about today, so she can afford to dream about tomorrow. We don't have that luxury. I care nothing for revolution. I care about surviving today. She can dare to risk and hope for change, but one day it will cost her, her head.

> (**MARIA** *appears in the doorway. She quickly moves to not be seen and eavesdrops.*)

SALLY. She's got courage. I'm gonna take my strength from that.

SOPHIE. *(laugh)* Fine then, come here and prostitute yourself as she has done. She talks of rights for women, living off of the men she sleeps with. How is that courage?

SALLY. She speaks what's on her mind. I'm tired of my own silence.

SOPHIE. As a slave in America you have achieved better than most. I warn you that as a woman in France there is no better, only a different version of the same thing.

SALLY. You earn your wage. You're not *owned*. I'm not lashed, no, but America's dripping with blood: with the blood of black slaves. And one day the soil will be so thick with it that each footstep you take will sink down into the earth, with all that blood seeping up, covering the bottom of everyone's shoes. And pretty soon all the land will be imprinted with 'em, with the bloody footprints of all our suffering. But everyone'll be walking 'round not noticing,' not seeing what they've all done. 'Cause they don't care. Right under their own feet. There'll be the proof of it. But it wont matter how much I point down and say, "See! See, what you've all done." 'Cause nobody's gonna care. And that'll just about kill me. So I don't want to stay there no longer.

SOPHIE. And soon, all of France will be set to blaze. Revolution is at hand. And its horror will be like nothing the world has ever seen. Madame *is* right about that. But revolution will not feed everyone soon enough. And the people who bring down the King in hopes of finally having some bread to eat will soon tear at each other for the leftover crumbs.

   (beat)

Think on it before you abandon one hell for another.

   *(**MARIA** reveals herself.)*

MARIA. Sophie, Madame De Gouges needs you in the dining room.

SOPHIE. Yes Miss.

   (She leaves. There is an awkward pause.)

SALLY. She's got foolish ideas.

MARIA. No, she's right. You can't do this.

SALLY. I'm doing nothing.

MARIA. But you will. I can see it.

(There is a moment of decision for SALLY; will she lie? She can't.)

SALLY. I can't go back. I can't.

MARIA. Have we hurt you so? I love you as my own sister.

SALLY. But I'm not your sister. I'm your slave. And I can't bear it anymore.

MARIA. We'll ask father to free you. I'll beg him. And Patsy? She'll do the same and then we can all be happy together again.

SALLY. *(laughs)* You are so… Even if your father did agree to free me, I can't stay in Virginia. You know it. It's the law. No freed slaves.

MARIA. So you'll go north. And I'll visit you. And – and look at you. With your skin no one will ever know you were a slave. We'll do great things.

SALLY. We're women. And the revolution that'll let us do great things won't happen while we're alive.

MARIA. You'll marry then. We'll find you some brilliant, successful man up north after you're free.

SALLY. No one will marry me.

MARIA. You're beautiful. You're skilled.

SALLY. And pregnant. Or have you forgotten?

(pause)

I know what lies down every road in America. France is an unknown. When there's an unknown, there's a possibility of somethin' good.

*(**SALLY** goes and takes the satchel and begins to pack.)*

I'll ask father to free your child. To free any child you have. He's never been able to refuse me. Your children will be free. Change happens quickly in America. Slavery can't last forever. Just think, it is already 1789. Can you imagine what their lives will be like when the next century comes? We'll all come back here to celebrate it. When they're younger even than you are now, they'll see Paris too but as free citizens. We'll all cheer the coming glories of the 19th century. And they'll come back to Monticello, not to serve us but to dine at our table. They'll see great things. They'll *do* great things. But not if you run away.

> *(Pause as **SALLY** stares at **MARIA** and contemplates what she has said. She picks up the satchel and begins unpacking it, putting the clothes back into the trunks. She breaks down crying, her decision leaving her in a whirlwind of mixed emotions. **MARIA** runs to embrace her.)*

Oh Sally... Shh...shh...shh...

> *(**MARTHA** enters.)*

MARTHA. Polly, lower your voice, we can hear you all the way from the dining – Oh my – ...What? What's the matter?

MARIA. Oh, it's nothing.

MARTHA. Sally, what's wrong? Polly what's happened here?

MARIA. Oh we were just finishing the packing. Chatting away about the glorious times we've had here. It's been lovely, hasn't it? Like a long beautiful vacation. We do so love Paris but I was telling Sally how much I've been missing home, how I couldn't wait to get back to Monticello, and she started crying out of joy with the thought of seeing it again.

> *(**MARTHA** goes to **SALLY** and holds her face in her hands.)*

MARTHA. I see.

> *(**SALLY** curls up in **MARTHA**'s lap and cries.)*

I see.

> *(We hear the sound of softly stomping feet. **SALLY** stands and faces the audience.)*

SALLY. Dear Thena. Sorry I haven't written in awhile. I hope all is well with everybody back at Monticello. Paris is still loud and it still feels like anything can happen anytime 'round any corner.

> *(Lights rise on the* **FRENCH MOB.** *The stomping begins gradually rising in volume.)*

But the noise of it all? It does sound different to me now.

> *(The* **CROWD** *starts whispering "Vive la liberte." It grows louder and louder in volume.)*

Things have changed since my last letter. Remember I was telling you about some dreams I was counting on? Well, my plans have changed. I'm coming home.

> *(She starts to cry.)*

I'm coming home.

FRENCH MOB. Vive la liberte! Vive la liberte! Vive la liberte! VIVE LA LIBERTE!!

> *(blackout)*

End of Play

Salat

SALAT was originally commissioned and produced in 2007 by Signature Theatre in Arlington, Virginia (Eric Schaeffer, Artistic Director, Maggie Boland, Managing Director) under the title EVE OF DESTRUCTION for their Signature in the Schools program (Marcia Gardner, Education Director). It was directed by Marcia Gardner, with choreography by Cassandra Jones with assistance from Matthew Gardiner, scenic design by Robert Perdziola, costume design by Allison Crawford, lighting design by Mark Lanks, and sound design by Tony Angelini. The cast was as follows:

WINSTON	Chris Stanton
CYNTHIA	Irene Casey
DANIEL	Graham Hooper
MR. REKERS	Ray Ficca
RASHA	Maria Wilson
RAQIM	Alan Dean Schiffer
FAHAD	Ben Truong
DANCERS	Jamil Garner, Kristin James

CHARACTERS

WINSTON – 16. American boy. A good student and a good friend.

RASHA – 16. Iraqi girl. Smart. Passionate. A dreamer.

RAQIM – 16. Iraqi boy. Smart. Focused. A true believer.

FAHAD – 16. Iraqi boy. Goes where the wind takes him.

CYNTHIA – 16. American girl. Way too smart for her own good.

DANIEL – 16. American boy. Struggling but working on it.

MR. REKERS – Early 40s. Daniel's father. Was blinded during Desert Storm. Trying to make it work against the odds.

DANCERS – Can be done with as many as you like but no fewer than three. They re-enact the stories told throughout the play. The style of these presentations should be very theatrical. Live musicians can be used if you have that option.

SETTING

The suburbs of an American city: March 2003
Basra, Iraq: March 2003
Basra, Iraq: February 1991
Sumer: 3000 BCE

(Darkness. We hear the recorded sounds of the Islamic call to prayer. It resonates throughout the theatre.)

(Lights rise on **WINSTON** *in a classroom giving a report. He speaks to the audience as if we were the class he is speaking to. There is a CD player next to him with speakers. The Islamic call to prayer now comes from the CD player. He looks at it proudly.)*

WINSTON. The Adhan *(Azaan)*:

(He looks at the audience.)

The Islamic call to prayer.

*(***RASHA** *runs on in secular, yet conservative dress, wearing a traditional hijab. She runs around the space, circling* **WINSTON** *— these two worlds seemingly together but totally apart — as* **RAQIM** *runs down a street in Basra followed lazily by his friend* **FAHAD** *who is leafing through a book.)*

RAQIM. Hurry up Fahad. We're going to be late for prayers.

(They continue their trek and circle around **WINSTON** *as he continues his presentation.)*

WINSTON. The five daily ritual prayers that Muslims offer to Allah — that's God — are called Salat.

(He holds up a cue card with the word Salat in bold letters written on it with the Arabic spelling next to it.)

"Salat." From the root Saad-Lam-Waw has the following meanings: prayer, supplication, petition, oration, eulogy, benediction, commendation, blessing, honor, magnify, bring forth, follow closely, walk or follow behind closely, to remain attached, to contact or to be in contact with. Its core underlying meaning relevant to all its usage in the Qur'an is to go or turn towards.

(We shift to **RASHA**. *She takes out a piece of paper and pencil from her pocket and begins to write.)*

RASHA. My dear American Friend:

(She contemplates what to write next as we shift back to **FAHAD** *as he catches up with* **RAQIM** *and reads from his book.)*

FAHAD. Here. Here. Listen. "It is not lawful for any woman who believes in Allah and the Last Day that she should uncover her hand more than this." *(He places his hand on his wrist joint.)* "When a woman reaches puberty *no part* of her body should remain uncovered except for her face… *(Beat as he realizes what he has just said. He continues disappointed.)* …and the hand up to the wrist joint."

RAQIM. *(laughs)* See? Mohammed never said women should cover their faces.

FAHAD. But – I… Wait. *(leafing through the book)* I know it's here somewhere. Here. Here. *(He reads from the book.)* "Some scholars are of the opinion that, because modern times are particularly full of mischief, women *should* go as far as to cover their faces because even the face may attract sexual glances from men."

RAQIM. *(joking)* Who have you been looking at Fahad?

FAHAD. *(ignoring the jab)* Scholars say, "We admit that the face is not one of the parts of the body to be covered, but it is not permissible for us to hold to this, taking into consideration the corruption of the modern age and the need to stop the means for further corruption."

RAQIM. You only hear what fits into what you believe.

(He grabs the book from **FAHAD** *and flips through it and finds the passage he wants.)*

Read.

*(He holds the book up to **FAHAD**, who reads from it:)*

FAHAD. Therefore, in the light of the Prophetic traditions it suffices to cover the body, leaving out the face and hands up to the wrist joints, since this is the specified Islamic covering...

*(**FAHAD** stops reading and sits, not wanting to go on. **RAQIM** sits next to him and shoves the book in his face, points at the page and reads.)*

RAQIM. ...and indeed it may sometimes be *essential* for a woman to go about her lawful engagements with her face *un*-covered.

*(We shift back to **RASHA** as she tries to figure out what to write next.)*

RASHA. My dear American Friend:

(She continues writing.)

The sun is just rising here. My father and brothers are at the Mosque for morning prayers and mother is cooking. Father thinks we're praying at home but Mother has too many chores. Father wants her to pray *and* to have food ready for him, but how can she do both? She and I never talk about it, so I guess it's what you call an "understanding" between us. She doesn't know I write to you but she does know sometimes I have to get out of the house, to...breathe some other air. I have so many letters for you now that I don't know how I can keep hiding them. Iraqi students are able to write to Americans but my father doesn't see any need for me to go to school anymore. I would just send them myself but I don't have the money for the postage and father will never give it to me. And even if I did, who would I address them to? "Friend. Care of the United States of America." But now you're coming to free us from Saddam. We are mostly Shiite here in Basra and we don't like him. After the last war many tried to rise up, my father among them. I was very young but I have memories of us hiding my father, and I can still call up visions of my friends crying because their fathers had been executed by Saddam's Republican Guard. We like freedom here, so we are happy you're coming. And that means I won't have to mail my letters. I will just give them to you. When you march into Basra I'll run up to each of you, one after another, shoving letters into your hands calling "Friend. Friend." Or maybe you'll arrive in jet planes and fall down from the sky like angels. And so, I will give my letters to a great bird like in the old stories.

>   *(Music. The actor playing the **GIANT BIRD** appears.)*

The bird will come and pick up the letters from my hand.

>   *(The **BIRD** picks up the single letter from **RASHA**'s hand and soars away with it. **RASHA** watches and follows in amazement.)*

And the bird will drop them lightly from its beak into your waiting hands and I will wave and wave from below up into the sky to all my floating American friends.

>   *(**RASHA** remembers something.)*

Oh! Can I tell you a secret?

>   *(The **BIRD** hovers with **RASHA**'s letter in hand. **RASHA** whispers in the **BIRD**'s ear.)*

RASHA & THE BIRD. *(**RASHA** starts and the **BIRD** echoes.)* It's best to come now. It is cooler now. If you wait too much longer it will soon get very hot. It is bad here when it is hot. You will not like it. Come now when the winds are cooler.

>   *(The **BIRD** flies off again with the letter. **RASHA** remembers something else and calls after the **BIRD**.)*

RASHA. Oh! One more thing.

>   *(The **BIRD** hovers again and **RASHA** whispers in her ear.)*

They say you are coming to find...to find...

> *(She cannot find the phrase.)*

THE BIRD. ...weapons of mass destruction.

RASHA. I haven't seen them, but if I do come across any, I'll write you again and tell you where they are.

> *(The BIRD glares at RASHA.)*

That was a joke.

> *(The BIRD takes the letter and rips it up into many pieces and soars away. RASHA runs after the BIRD.)*

No!

> *(We shift back to RAQIM and FAHAD.)*

RAQIM. We have to go. We're late.

> *(We shift back to WINSTON and we hear a voice calling to him.)*

CYNTHIA. Winston...? Winston...?

> *(WINSTON starts flipping through his index cards in a panic.)*

WINSTON. Wait, okay?

CYNTHIA. You screwed up.

WINSTON. I did not.

CYNTHIA. You started wrong. This is my part.

> *(We shift back to RASHA as she battles with the BIRD.)*

RASHA. What have you done? What have you done?!

> *(We shift back to FAHAD running after RAQIM.)*

FAHAD. It's your fault. Why couldn't you just agree with me? Why can't you ever agree?

> *(CYNTHIA walks up to WINSTON.)*

CYNTHIA. You didn't start at the right place, so now we're all off track.

(**FAHAD** *chases after* **RAQIM**.)

FAHAD. And give me back my book!

WINSTON. Things can change Cynthia. Plans can change.

    (**CYNTHIA** *grabs for the cards.*)

CYNTHIA. Gimme.

WINSTON. You need to breathe.

CYNTHIA. We need to start over.

    (**RAQIM** *stops and faces* **FAHAD**.)

RAQIM. Just think Fahad, if everyone agreed all the time, then the Americans wouldn't be coming, and then who would we hate?

    (*He tosses the book in the air and* **FAHAD** *laughs as he catches it. At the same time the* **BIRD** *tosses the ripped up letter into the air and* **RASHA** *grasps into the air for the fluttering tiny pieces of paper.*)

RASHA. No, no, no, no, no…

    (**WINSTON** *holds the cards above* **CYNTHIA**'s *head. She grabs for the cards and he lets go of them, letting them flutter to the ground.*)

WINSTON. Oops.

CYNTHIA. Mrs. Litvinis can we go back? We were supposed to start with this.

    (*A huge map of Iraq falls behind* **WINSTON** *and* **CYNTHIA** *blocking our view of* **RASHA**, *the* **BIRD**, **RAQIM**, *and* **FAHAD**. **DANIEL** *sits asleep in class.* **WINSTON** *continues.*)

WINSTON. So. Iraq – (*He points at the map behind him.*)

    (*He tries to continue the presentation while* **CYNTHIA** *scrambles for the cards on the floor while posing her argument to their teacher.*)

CYNTHIA. He got it wrong. He was supposed to do the introduction, and then the map was supposed to come down and I was going to come up and Winston was going to talk about religion and writing and books while I provided visual aids, he and I back and forth, then we'd do a lead-in to Daniel and he'd go and then we'd go back to me and then all three of us were going to join together and do a big finish – but Winston had to go and mess it all –

WINSTON. I had my cards mixed up, ok?

CYNTHIA. It was going to be impressive. Structurally. It was going to be very different than most reports. Don't you see the innovation? The going back and forth? Instead of just subject, subject, subject, we were going to be more fluid and everyone would have been more interested than usual and we would have gotten an A, but Winston had to go and mess it up!

> *(She breaks down crying. **WINSTON** stares at her. She stops. **WINSTON** goes back to the report.)*

WINSTON. Iraq –

> *(**CYNTHIA** points at the map.)*

– is the site of ancient Mesopotamia where the first recorded civilization was located. These ancient people were called Sumerians.

> *(**CYNTHIA** takes a cut out of a Sumerian and sticks it onto the map.)*

This area was known as the "Cradle of Civilization."

> *(**CYNTHIA** hits the CD player and we hear a baby's cry.)*

The Sumerians invented written language almost six thousand years ago. The language was written with a reed –

> *(**CYNTHIA** holds up a reed.)*

– on clay tablets –

> *(**CYNTHIA** holds up a Styrofoam tablet.)*

– in a script called cuneiform.

> (**CYNTHIA** *demonstrates writing on the tablet with the reed.*)

The first libraries consisted of stacks of these clay tablets. Recording of poetry, epics, and history were begun by the Sumerians. Perhaps the oldest recorded story –

> (**CYNTHIA** *turns the tablets toward the class and it has some rustic illustration on it.*)

CYNTHIA. – Lugalbanda: The Boy Who Got Caught Up in a War, –

WINSTON. – was found during the 19th century –

> (**CYNTHIA** *puts on a pith helmet and holds up a pick axe.*)

CYNTHIA. *(gasps)* Eureka!

WINSTON. – but was not deciphered until the 1970s.

> (**CYNTHIA** *puts on sunglasses.* **WINSTON** *holds up the tablets for* **CYNTHIA** *to read.*)

CYNTHIA. Groovy.

WINSTON. This story is older than the Torah –

> (**CYNTHIA** *holds up a miniature Torah in one hand.*)

– the Bible –

> (**CYNTHIA** *holds up a crucifix in the other hand.*)

– and the Qu'ran –

> (**WINSTON** *hits the CD player and we hear a quick snippet of the Islamic call to prayer.*)

It's older than Homer or the Greek and Roman myths.

CYNTHIA. Sumer.

> (**WINSTON** *glares at her again.*)

WINSTON. Yes. Ancient Sumer.

> (*Music. Lights rise behind the Iraq map allowing it to function like scrim. As* **WINSTON** *continues, we see the following enacted – bending toward abstraction – by dancers.*)

Sumer lay on a hot flat plain, between two great rivers, the Tigris and Euphrates. The land itself was not rich or welcoming to any living thing for it suffered daily as it baked in the sun. But the Sumerians were a skilled people. They dug canals to carry the river waters out over the dry, dead, earth. They planted. And soon there were vines heavy with ripe fruit and vegetables tearing up through rich soil. Herbs and spices scented the air. And tall palms dropped dates onto flocks of sheep, cows, and goats that grazed around the apple, fig and pomegranate trees below. They took clay from the ground making pots and paving roads and building cities that towered over the river plains. And so it was, almost five thousand years ago, on the very same clay that built temples to their gods and palaces for their kings, that our story, the very first story –

CYNTHIA. – Lugalbanda: The Boy Who Got Caught Up in a War, –

WINSTON. – a story that had been passed from storyteller to storyteller for longer than anyone could remember, came to be written down.

> *(Pause. **WINSTON** and **CYNTHIA** wait. Clearly something is supposed to happen. They look around nervously. **CYNTHIA** clears her throat to try to wake the sleeping **DANIEL**. **WINSTON** whispers to him.)*

Hey... Hey Daniel, it's time.

> *(**WINSTON** looks up toward the class and his teacher in the back. He looks to **CYNTHIA** who seems paralyzed with fear.)*

Ummm...

> *(**WINSTON** tries to fake his way through.)*

Yeah. Ummm...

> *(He flips through the index cards.)*

This wasn't my part.

> *(He looks at the sleeping **DANIEL** again.)*

(whispering) Hey. Hey.

CYNTHIA. DANIEL!

(**DANIEL** *wakes up startled.*)

DANIEL. What? What?!

CYNTHIA. (*She raises her hand.*) Mrs. Litvinis this is just wrong. Daniel's been a problem from the very beginning, from our very first study group meeting. I had it all planned out. I was going to do the section on *The Boy Who Got Caught Up In a War* 'cause I like to read. I like books. I always have. I'm a good reader. It made sense. Winston is a Catholic so there you go: religion. He would do religion. And I said Daniel should do the section on the first Gulf War, but he didn't want to do that, and we had to have him do something, so I gave up the Lugalbanda section, cause I'm cooperative, I am, I do stuff like that, that's just the way I am, and now *he's* gone and messed it all up. He should have done the Gulf War section like I suggested 'cause it made perfect sense – all of us talking about what we know. I mean his father went over there the first time, right?

WINSTON. Cynthia –

CYNTHIA. But I was like, "Fine, I'll do it, but I am asking your dad to come in and talk," and Daniel just like freaked out which is a real shame because here we are going over there again and if Mr. Rekers had come in and talked, we could have had some historical perspective. If Daniel would have just been helpful and asked his father to come in, we would have had a personal first hand account of like, war.

(*Lights up on* **MR. REKERS**, **DANIEL**'s *father in 1991 dressed in fatigues writing a letter home.*)

MR. REKERS. (*a call like a werewolf*) Aaooooooooo!!!! Well son, this morning I woke up and heard the *second* best news since I've been here – Our President, Mr. George Herbert Walker Bush announcing a bona fide cease-fire. And then I was working on patients later in the morning when, so help me, I heard the *very* best news since I've been here- that Iraq had accepted the cease-fire terms. So that's it. Invasion – bam – victory. One of the guys I was fixing up today said, "We're gonna have to come back," but I say we've done our job, and if we've screwed up and made a mistake and didn't finish it and left the Iraqis with a much bigger problem by not killing off Saddam – If that's short sighted on our part, well I'm sorry, it's the rebels job to finish what we started, and all I know is, I'm outta here, and pretty soon you'll be tackling me again in the backyard.

Sometimes Danny, I wish you could see what I'm seeing. Like right now, as I write this, the sun is setting, and to the south I can see the red glow of an oil field burning under dark Kuwaiti skies, with a full moon rising above the clouds. And even though I know the tragedy of why and how such a sight exists, I gotta tell you, the actual composition of the vision – the light and dark and mix of colors – can only be called beautiful. Give Mommy a kiss for me, and I'll see you soon. Love Dad.

*(Lights down on **MR. REKERS** and back up on the classroom.)*

CYNTHIA. I'm sorry but Daniel's laziness and negligence shouldn't affect my grade. If he would have had his father come in and talk to us, then we would have gotten a good grade, but now we'll probably fail and my GPA will plummet and I'll never get into a good school and my life will be over and it's all your fault Daniel Rekers, so what do you have to say for yourself?

*(**DANIEL** gets up lazily from his desk and goes up to the Iraq map, turns, and addresses the class.)*

DANIEL. My father went to war twelve years ago. I don't remember him going and I don't remember him being gone. I don't know what it was like for him over there. I don't know anything about over there. All I know is that there was some sort of an explosion and he came back blind. He tried to act like everything was normal and that he was just a normal father and that we could do normal father/son stuff, so he tried to throw a football to me when I was ten and it hit me in the face and it cut my cheek, which is why I have this stupid scar.

(He starts to go back and sit down, but then goes back to stand in front of the Iraq map instead.)

Oh yeah. I hope we blow that whole country off the map this time around. The end.

(He grabs the map and yanks it down. Behind the map we see his father, **MR. REKERS**, *at home reading a book in brail.)*

MR. REKERS. In the land of Sumer, in the city of Uruk there was a great King. And the King decided to make war against his rival city Aratta, and he aimed to destroy it and plunder it for all its riches. And the King had sons – eight sons who were the captains of his armies.

(Lights rise on **FAHAD** *reading a book.)*

MR. REKERS & FAHAD. And his youngest son was named Lugalbanda.

(As **DANIEL** *arrives home from school, we see* **RAQIM** *running up to* **FAHAD**. *He is a little out of breath.)*

RAQIM & DANIEL. What are you reading?

FAHAD. I – …I – …I found it with your things.

MR. REKERS. When Winston and Cynthia were over talking about your project, I ordered it so I could give it a read. It's good stuff.

DANIEL. Whatever.

MR. REKERS. So, how did it go today?

DANIEL. How'd what go?

MR. REKERS. The project. Your presentation?

DANIEL. Oh. Fine.

MR. REKERS. Yeah?

DANIEL. Yeah. Jeez.

MR. REKERS. You know, I could come in and talk to your class. I could do it on a day when I'm not teaching. I'd like to. I was kinda hoping that you'd ask me to.

DANIEL. Yeah, well I didn't.

*(He goes to his room as we see **RAQIM** grabs the book from **FAHAD**.)*

RAQIM. I thought you only read Qur'an.

FAHAD. I do but – …You won't tell my father will you?

RAQIM. Of course not.

FAHAD. So do they go to war?

RAQIM. What?

FAHAD. In the story.

RAQIM. I don't have time for that now. I have to tell you something.

FAHAD. Alright.

RAQIM. Not here. It's a secret. No one can know.

*(He drags **FAHAD** off. Lights up on **RASHA** secretly writing another letter.)*

RASHA. My Dear American Friend – As each new day comes I wake thinking, "This is it. This is the day when the Americans will come." It gives me a hope to wake up to every morning and a wish to fall asleep with every night. Would it be possible for you to bring me some books? I know we have our own Arab writers, like Naguib Mahfouz and Nazik al-Malaika, but I've read those stories so often that I feel like one of the old storytellers, telling the tale over and over until it can't be erased from the mind. I want – I need something new to fill my head. I would like to read the great stories from around the world. I want to know of Mr. Dickens, and of Mr. Tolstoy, and of your Mark Twain. Oh, what tales I hear they tell.

*(Lights come up on **DANIEL** at home answering his cell phone and **WINSTON** outside school on his cell phone.)*

WINSTON. Hey.
DANIEL. Hey.

>   *(pause)*

WINSTON. So what's up?
DANIEL. Nothing.
WINSTON. Ok.
DANIEL. Yeah.
WINSTON. Cool.

>   *(pause)*

DANIEL. Sorry about today…
WINSTON. Oh. Yeah.
DANIEL. Yeah.

>   *(pause)*

WINSTON. So when do you think you can finish it?
DANIEL. What?
WINSTON. The story.
DANIEL. What?

>   *(**CYNTHIA** seemingly appears out of thin air and grabs the phone from **WINSTON**.)*

CYNTHIA. Look, Litvinis will give us an extension.
DANIEL. Aw jeez.
CYNTHIA. Just do it Daniel 'cause she's only giving us a one day extension, so go on the internet and look up the story, and start now because its not going to be easy 'cause its like directly translated from the Sumerian, so you have to put it into your own words, and I can't do it for you because I'm too good of a writer and Litvinis would know right away that it was me, and don't say "Just write it like I would" because that would be way too hard because you can't write and I am not going to weaken my mental abilities by sinking down to your level of intelligence, and don't even think of asking Winston 'cause he has band practice. Bye.

(She hands the phone to **WINSTON** *and she walks off.)*

WINSTON. Sorry.

DANIEL. Yeah.

WINSTON. So?

DANIEL. Alright.

WINSTON. Cool.

DANIEL. Yeah.

WINSTON. Bye.

DANIEL. Cya.

(They both hang up. Lights up on **RAQIM** *pulling* **FAHAD** *along.)*

FAHAD. What is going on?

(He pulls away from **RAQIM.***)*

RAQIM. No one can know.

FAHAD. Fine. Tell me.

RAQIM. You know the great library.

FAHAD. Of course.

RAQIM. I just heard that the librarian there has been asking permission to move all the books from the library to keep them from being destroyed when the Americans and British come, but the Governor won't let her do it. Don't you see? It'll all be gone – the history of Basra will be gone.

FAHAD. And you want to help her?

RAQIM. They'll come and the city will burn and so will all the books, every single great story.

FAHAD. Every story?

RAQIM. Yes! Aren't you listening to me?

FAHAD. She is Shiite. Is she going to save the stories of Saddam. Are his stories even in the library? As a Sunni, if the Americans do come, you should be more worried about saving yourself from the Shiite's than in saving some old books.

RAQIM. Fahad, in the Qur'an the first thing that Allah said to Muhammad was "*Read.*" We have to do something.

FAHAD. What?

RAQIM. We're not boys anymore. There are moments to test yourself, to decide who you are and what you believe.

>   (*beat*)

FAHAD. Jihad.

RAQIM. Yes. Jihad.

>   (*Blackout. Sounds of explosions. The dancers or the entire cast read overlapping news annoucements.*)

ANNOUNCER. At approximately 5:30 AM Iraqi local time explosions were heard in Baghdad.

At 10:15pm, Eastern Standard Time, President George W. Bush announced that he has ordered the coalition to launch an "attack of opportunity" against specified targets in Iraq.

More than 40 satellite-guided Tomahawk cruise missiles have been launched from U.S. warships in the Red Sea and Persian Gulf, "surgically" striking a bunker in Baghdad believed to be holding top Iraqi officials.

President Bush said in addressing the nation, "On my orders, coalition forces have begun striking selected targets of military importance to undermine Saddam Hussein's ability to wage war."

>   (*Lights rise on* **MR. REKERS** *listening to the newscast.*)

"These are opening stages of what will be a broad and concerted campaign."

"The military action is being dubbed "Operation Iraqi Freedom".

>   (**DANIEL** *comes downstairs and heads for the front door.*)

DANIEL. Cya later.

MR. REKERS. Where are you going?

DANIEL. Winston's.

MR. REKERS. He has band practice.

DANIEL. I'm meeting him after.

MR. REKERS. Oh, so you know, he's not helping you with your assignment.

DANIEL. Are you listening to my calls?

MR. REKERS. Tell Cynthia she needs to talk quieter.

DANIEL. I'm outta here.

MR. REKERS. Sit down!

> (*DANIEL stops in his tracks never having heard this tone from his father.*)

You're angry I know.

DANIEL. I'm not ang –

MR. REKERS. You've been angry since you were five years old.

DANIEL. I am not angry.

MR. REKERS. No, you're pissed off. You should be Danny, and –

DANIEL. Don't call me that.

MR. REKERS. Fine. Daniel. I went over there and came back someone different, and I wish I could change it, but I can't. I wish your mother hadn't left but…

DANIEL. Don't go there.

MR. REKERS. Hey!

> (*beat*)

You know, I used to write you letters when I was over there. We were saving them for you, but after the divorce I couldn't find where your mother had put them.

DANIEL. Well, letters are easy to lose I guess.

MR. REKERS. Yeah.

DANIEL. She probably took them with her like everything else.

MR. REKERS. Don't go blaming your mother.

DANIEL. No, I'll leave that to you!

MR. REKERS. Look!

> *(beat)*

People say things, in the moment that they don't mean. Some people can't…bear the weight that things will never be the… It'd be nice if when spouses saw their husbands or wives with an arm or leg miss – …or gone blind, or just depressed enough to not want to get out of bed in the morning. It'd be nice if there was unconditional love – for richer, for poorer, in sickness and in health, but people who love one another fail each other all the time, sometimes when it matters most.

DANIEL. Yeah, I noticed. And she got to walk out and I'm stuck here.

MR. REKERS. Yeah, you're stuck here.

DANIEL. Why?!

MR. REKERS. Because she left both of us!

> *(beat)*

You and me. War buddies. I used to wonder in the hospital before I came back, "How am I gonna stand not being able to see my own son look me in the eyes?" But I never prepared myself for the fact that you would totally *stop* looking.

DANIEL. Jeez! Do you have to be so dramatic about –

MR. REKERS. I can hear your breath. The direction of your breath. And it never comes toward me.

DANIEL. Whatever.

> *(**DANIEL** turns and walks away from his father.)*

MR. REKERS. You're facing away from me now.

DANIEL. Uh… Duh.

> *(A beat. **DANIEL** is going to test his father. He turns his head to his left.)*

MR. REKERS. Left.

> *(**DANIEL** turns his head to the right.)*

Right.

(**DANIEL** *lifts his head quickly upwards.*)

Up.

(**DANIEL** *turns his head to even quicker to his left and then quickly down.*)

Left, down.

(**DANIEL** *is a little freaked out.*)

DANIEL. That's just good luck. You're guessing.

MR. REKERS. I can't see you Daniel. But I can feel you. You're my son. And if you'll notice, you still haven't looked straight at me.

(**DANIEL** *slowly walks up to his father and gets right in his face.*)

DANIEL. You're full of crap. Talking to me like you suddenly have all this wisdom. Where was it back when you came across that landmine, huh dad? Where was it when Mom took you for everything you had? My dad: the wise one. Like Yoda or something.

MR. REKERS. Now that's my son.

(**DANIEL** *goes to leave.*)

So. Here we go.

DANIEL. Aw jeez! I don't know where *you're* going, but I'm leaving.

MR. REKERS. Things are changing.

DANIEL. Yeah, yeah, I know – the world is changing, blah, blah, blah. America is at war.

MR. REKERS. And the Cold War in this house just ended. We just went to battle. SO, SIT DOWN!

(**DANIEL** *does instinctively.*)

Now. I haven't been a very good father. Too lenient. Too easy. Too sorry for you and for myself. So we're gonna start simple.

(*He picks up his brail book of* **LUGALBANDA.**)

I'm gonna help you with your assignment. We're gonna read.

DANIEL. I don't want to read anything that has anything to do with those terrorist nutcases over in that loser country.

MR. REKERS. You –! ...got a lot to learn

> (**MR. REKERS** *opens the book and begins to read from it – the story unfolds in front of our eyes with help from the dancers.*)

The armies of the King led by his eight sons traveled toward Aratta through the cold, treacherous, mountains.

> (*Lights rise on* **RAQIM** *with a satchel followed by* **FAHAD**, *with a shovel, walking along a street in Basra at night.* **MR. REKERS** *continues reading the story as* **RAQIM** *tells* **FAHAD** *the rest of the tale.*)

They were halfway along their journey when a sickness fell upon the youngest prince.

FAHAD. Lugalbanda?

RAQIM. Yes. Lugalbanda the King's youngest son.

FAHAD. Then what happened?

MR. REKERS & RAQIM. The little prince –

MR. REKERS. – jerked like a snake dragged by its head with a reed –

RAQIM. – like a gazelle caught in a snare.

MR. REKERS. No longer could his hands return the grip of his father's touch –

RAQIM. – or lift his foot to take but a tiny step.

MR. REKERS. Neither his father –

FAHAD. The King?

RAQIM. Yes, the King.

MR. REKERS. Nor his brothers –

RAQIM. Nor any there with them could ease his pain or vanquish his ailment.

MR. REKERS. They talked of bringing him to safety in the cities of Unug or Kulaba, but as they debated the safest route, the prince's teeth chattered with so hard a fury that those there who loved him feared they might shatter in the cold mountain air.

FAHAD. Teeth can't shatter. I don't care how cold it is.

   (**RAQIM** *stops walking and points to the side of the road.*)

RAQIM. Dig.

   (**FAHAD** *starts digging as the story continues.*)

MR. REKERS. They found a warm cave for him there in the mountains and they made him an arbor like a birds nest to rest and recover in. And Lugalbanda's eyes stayed open, staring straight out at those all around him with water flooding from his eyes. And that gave all who waited there hope. But his lips did not open to his brothers' cries no matter how hard they begged him to give but a hint of life. When they lifted his neck, there was no breath there any longer, and so the King and his sons laid out cheese and sweetmeats and baskets of dates and eggs and rolls with butter and beer for drinking. And they placed by his head his axe of tin, and upon his chest his dagger made of iron.

   (**FAHAD** *stops digging.*)

FAHAD. Wait.

DANIEL. Whoa.

MR. REKERS & RAQIM. What?

DANIEL. That's it?

FAHAD. They're just going to leave him there?

MR. REKERS. They offered him the best they could.

RAQIM. If he dies then he'll have a proper burial and have provisions for the afterlife and if he lives he'll have what he needs to survive in the mountains. It's very smart actually.

MR. REKERS. So the King and his sons and their armies went on their way out of the mountains and away from the hidden cave. Days passed and Lugalbanda did not rouse from his sickness. Finally he raised his eyes to heaven, to Utu. And in the mountain cave the little prince raised to him his fair hands and wept to him as if to his own father.

> (**MR. REKERS** *stops reading; the wording of the story is a little too close to home for him.*)

DANIEL. What?

MR. REKERS. Umm…

> (**RAQIM** *takes the shovel from* **FAHAD**.)

RAQIM. Come on, we need to hurry.

FAHAD. You're not going to finish the story?

MR. REKERS. I'm a little tired. It's your assignment. You can finish on your own.

RAQIM. We don't have time.

DANIEL. Oh… Ok.

> (*He heads upstairs.*)

MR. REKERS. 'Night.

DANIEL. Yeah.

> (*Lights down on them as* **RAQIM** *takes out the satchel and unwraps it. Inside is his copy of* **LUGALBANDA**.)

FAHAD. What?!

RAQIM. Come on, we need to hurry before our parents figure out we're gone.

FAHAD. This was the big plan? This was the secret mission? This is our act of jihad?!

RAQIM. Yes. As a sign of support and solidarity, with the librarian of Basra. We can't let them take our culture from us. What did you think we were going to do?

FAHAD. Plant a roadside bomb?

> (**RAQIM** *bursts into laughter and then it fades when he sees that* **FAHAD** *is not laughing.*)

RAQIM. You thought…? Really? How…? Why…?

FAHAD. The Americans are coming. We have to be ready for them.

RAQIM. But –

FAHAD. You hate them. You say it all the time, "They will come and destroy all that we were, all that we are." They're already dropping bombs on Baghdad like they're throwing stones on an anthill. And when they invade, it'll be by land. They'll come from the sea and head toward Baghdad, and they'll wipe out everything in their way. Basra will be first.

(RAQIM can only look at his friend.)

When they strike at us, we have to strike back. It's the only way.

(RAQIM cannot answer.)

(the sound of explosions and gunfire in the distance)

RAQIM. What was that?

FAHAD. It's begun. They're here.

(Lights down on them as lights rise on RASHA.)

RASHA. My Dear American friend – In the outskirts of Basra Iraqi militias are fighting with the Americans and the British. Baghdad is burning. We hear there are many dead there. You'll stop soon, won't you? We Iraqi people don't want war, Sunni, Shiite, whether we support Saddam or not, we want peace, so please, I ask you, as my dearest friend, stop the killing. The civilians do nothing wrong. It will do nothing to kill them. You want Saddam right? Kill him. And leave the rest alone. This I ask you – beg of you. Your Iraqi friend, Rasha

(We hear a school bell ring. WINSTON is sitting, reading a worn copy of On the Road *in the hall outside the classroom. DANIEL comes up and just stands next to him. There is a longish pause as they say nothing. Finally DANIEL sits next to WINSTON.)*

DANIEL. Hey.
WINSTON. Hey.
DANIEL. So I finished it.
WINSTON. Yeah?
DANIEL. Yeah.

> *(pause as they just sit there)*

It's kind of a cool story.
WINSTON. Yeah.
DANIEL. Yeah.

> *(pause as they just sit there)*

So he like, goes off to war with his brothers and stuff.
WINSTON. Yeah.

> *(beat)*

DANIEL. Would you?
WINSTON. What?
DANIEL. Well, go to war.
WINSTON. Naw.
DANIEL. What if we like, had to?
WINSTON. Go to war?
DANIEL. Yeah.
WINSTON. You mean the draft?
DANIEL. Yeah.
WINSTON. No way. Never happen. People would like, rise up.
DANIEL. But what if it happened anyway? What if you had to like, go and kill people and be brave and stuff?
WINSTON. Well, it's not gonna happen, so don't worry about it. People would start talking. Yelling maybe. *(holding up his book)* People used to say stuff. About what was going on. About what they were, you know, feeling. How they felt about stuff. If there was a draft, I think that might happen again. You know marching in the streets. Saying, like… "No."

DANIEL. Hm.

(beat)

WINSTON. Makes me wonder though – who's actually going over there? I mean who are they getting to volunteer? I mean besides your dad, but that was back then. The first time around.

DANIEL. He wanted to go. You know like duty and apple pie and stuff.

WINSTON. Hm.

DANIEL. Yeah.

(pause as they just sit there)

I don't know if I could.

WINSTON. What?

DANIEL. Go to war like him.

WINSTON. Like who?

DANIEL. My dad.

WINSTON. Ah.

(pause as they just sit there)

DANIEL. Couldn't have been easy.

WINSTON. Nope.

DANIEL. Never really thought about it. Couldn't have been easy at all.

*(Lights up on **RASHA**.)*

RASHA. My dear American friend – There's been an uprising. Many Shiites are now fighting the Iraqi militias. My father is among them. This is our chance he says. Saddam will fall and Iraq will be ours again. But still, I wish it would stop. My city doesn't look the same. We have to stay in most of the time because of the fighting and the looting, which is why what I did tonight is hard to believe. My stack of letters is so high that I can't hide them in my room anymore so tonight I snuck out.

*(We see this re-enacted by a dancer dressed as **RASHA** as **RASHA** herself narrates the tale.)*

I dug into the ground. I clawed and scraped with my bare hands, and as I got deeper my hand hit something hard. And as I looked down and squinted into the darkness I saw a book.

*(The dancer playing the **RASHA** double lifts the copy of **LUGALBANDA** into the air.)*

Thank you for bringing it to me. I knew you wouldn't fail me. Your friend, Rasha

*(The dancer playing the **RASHA** double puts the stack of letters into the hole and buries them and then runs off with the book.)*

Oh, one last thing. I ask of you again to stop the fighting. I thought we were friends, so why won't you do me this favor? I know you've sent the book but I would gladly trade it for peace.

*(**FAHAD** comes out of the shadows, starts to dig, and lifts the stack of letters out of the ground. He runs off.)*

*(The sound of a school bell. **DANIEL** is in front of the class. He is in the middle of his story. As he tells it we see the dancers bring it to life.)*

DANIEL. With the help of the gods Lugalbanda grew strong again but he did not know his way out of the mountains. And then he thought –

LUGALBANDA. "Maybe the great bird can help me? Maybe Anzud will lead me to my brothers, my father, and his armies."

DANIEL. So the little prince set out to find the great bird's nest.

*(Lights up on **RAQIM** reading a book. **FAHAD** comes up to him.)*

FAHAD. Raqim, you never told me the end of that story.

RAQIM. Which story?

FAHAD. The one about the boy who got caught up in a war.

RAQIM. *(laugh)* You know where it is. Go back and dig it up and read it yourself.

FAHAD. I thought the whole idea was to hide the book.

RAQIM. Yes, but…you know, I searched out the Librarian of Basra and I've met her. She laughed when I told her what I did. I told her I would bring her the book for safer keeping, but she said, "No, what you've done is noble. And we shouldn't hide books. We should only keep them safe. Your book is safe for now, and if someone finds it, then they'll read the story and remember it and hopefully they'll pass it on to someone else."

RAQIM. So go read it Fahad, and then pass it on to someone else.

FAHAD. It's gone.

RAQIM. What?

FAHAD. I did go there to read it. But someone else found it before I did. A girl. And she left these.

(He holds up the stack of letters.)

You should read them. The subject matter is very interesting. I bet I could make money with these or at least cause a lot of trouble for her and her American loving family if I told about them.

*(Lights up on **RASHA**.)*

RASHA. My dear American friend – There's sad news today. I was at home when I heard screaming from the street. There was a crowd of people, my mother at the front, and they were all covered in blood. At first I thought, "Was there a bomb?" And then I saw. They were carrying my father's body, and the blood on their clothes wasn't their own. We don't know who shot him. There is so much confusion here. I went to my mother asking, "Was it the militia? Was it Saddam?" And she looked at me wild-eyed and screaming, "American! American!" But we really don't know. All day I've blamed myself for his death because of all the horrible things I've done: lying to my father, writing to you when I should have been praying, taking that book from the ground, and sometimes wishing he was gone so I could go back to school. I prayed today, all five times. It's good that the letters are buried. I'm going to return your book back to the ground and bury this letter and the one before with the rest of them. I have to forget you because as I write this, all I can hear is my mother's voice, "American! American!" and I sit here thinking, "Even if an American didn't pull the trigger, my father wouldn't be dead if the American's hadn't come." Forgive me. Your friend, Rasha

*(Lights down on her as they rise on **FAHAD** and **RAQIM**.)*

RAQIM. You're going to give me those letters.

FAHAD. No I'm not.

RAQIM. You're going to give them to me and you're never going to speak of them again.

FAHAD. Why not?

RAQIM. Because you're Muslim.

FAHAD. I am Iraqi.

RAQIM. You are Muslim. And you would never allow yourself to cause someone such horrible pain.

*(**RAQIM** holds out his hand. **FAHAD** hands him the letters. Lights go down on them as the rise on **DANIEL** continuing his story in front of the class as we see it enacted by the dancers.)*

DANIEL. Lugalbanda found the nest but Anzud was not there, only the great bird's chick was in the nest. Lugalbanda went back to his cave and brought cakes and honey and salt meat and sheep fat, and decorated the nest with sprigs of white cedar and painted the young birds eyes as if he were a king. When Anzud returned and found Lugalbanda and saw what he had done, the great bird offered the little prince anything he desired. Lugalbanda looked to the bird and spoke:

LUGALBANDA. Put the power of running in my thighs. Let them never grow tired. Moving like the sunlight, like the goddess Inana, let me leap like flame and blaze like lightning! Wherever I look, allow me to go. Wherever I cast my glance, there let me set my foot. Wherever my heart desires, there let me reach, and let me loosen my shoes in whatever place my heart dares to name.

DANIEL. And all the bird asked in return was that when Lugalbanda returned to his city that the little prince would have the wood carvers fashion statues of the great bird. And Lugalbanda replied,

LUGALBANDA. "You will be breathtaking to look upon. Your name will be made famous thereby in Sumer and your likeness will be a credit to the temples of the great gods. Now great bird, show me. Show me to my father. Lead me with your keen sight."

DANIEL. And the bird flew up into the skies and the little prince ran faster than the light passing through a flickering eyelid until finally the great bird stopped, and looked down to see Lugalbanda run into this father's arms.

> *(Lights down on **DANIEL** as they rise on **RASHA** with the book digging into the earth. She cannot find her letters. She digs more frantically. **RAQIM** steps out of the shadows with her stack of letters.)*

RAQIM. Are you looking for these?

RASHA. Who are you?

RAQIM. Well, I'm the owner of that book in your hand for one thing.

RASHA. I didn't steal it. I found it here, and –

RAQIM. How about a trade? It seems we both found something that the other was trying to hide.

> *(He hands out the letters to her. **RASHA** doesn't take them.)*

RAQIM. Don't hide them here. It's not safe. Take them.

RASHA. I don't want them anymore.

RAQIM. Then why were you hiding them?

RASHA. I can do what I like with them.

RAQIM. But if you don't want them anymore –

RASHA. I don't. Too much has changed. I can't believe the girl who wrote them is me.

RAQIM. Why?

RASHA. Because I don't feel the same way toward – about – …Why do you ask so many questions?

RAQIM. I'm sorry. You're a good writer.

> *(No one has ever said such a thing to her. He hands the letters out again. **RASHA** stares at him and slowly takes the letters.)*

Where do you study?

RASHA. I don't go to school.

RAQIM. Why not?

RASHA. I've had enough schooling.

RAQIM. You can never have enough schooling.

RASHA. My father –

RAQIM. Oh, I don't want to hear this. If he doesn't want you to go then you should disobey him. Iraqis are an educated people. These American's thinking they're saving us, bringing down Saddam when *he* was the one who saved us. He said, "We will read. Illiteracy will be wiped from Iraq's borders." He made education free for all of us. And so what's going to happen if they pull him down? We'll all be peasants again left to kill each other. You're a writer. You could be a great writer for our country. You can't keep it hidden in those letters. If your father doesn't see that, then he's an –

RASHA. Don't speak of my father. He is – …was…

RAQIM. Oh… Oh, I see.

> *(long pause)*

(pointing to the book) Did you like the story?

RASHA. Oh. Yes.

(awkward pause as neither knows what to say)

I envy him. Lugalbanda. Going off to war. Fighting for his people. I envy you the same thing. It's not fair that I can't be a soldier.

RAQIM. But he wasn't really a soldier on the front lines in the end. That's not how he helped. He was in the background, helping the cause of his people. Listen.

*(He grabs the book from her and reads as we see **DANIEL** in front of the class continuing his presentation as we see the dancers enact the story.)*

DANIEL. "And so Lugalbanda returned to his father and he camped with the King's armies outside the walls of Aratta, and from the city it rained down javelins as if from the clouds, and sling-stones numerous as the raindrops falling in a whole year whizzed down loudly from Arrata's walls. They were trapped by their enemies on one side and the treacherous mountains on the other.

*(**MR. REKERS** reads the story to himself at home.)*

MR. REKERS. The King sought someone whom he could send back to his city but no one said to him "I will go to the city." From his most elite troops to his lowest foot soldiers, there was silence.

DANIEL. Then Lugalbanda alone arose from the ranks.

LUGALBANDA. "My king, I will go to the city, but no one shall go with me."

DANIEL. And the King said –

MR. REKERS. "Go my son and speak to Inana the keeper of the sun, who shades herself in the halls of my earthly palace and ask her why she has forsaken me. Ask for her divine guidance and help."

DANIEL. And so from the foot of the mountains, through the high passes, down into the flat lands, Lugalbanda crossed five, six, seven mountains until finally he set foot joyfully in the city of his birth. Inana of the sun, sat there on her cushion. He bowed and prostrated himself on the ground. He had only to speak and his task was finished. Looking upon her face he knew all would be well."

(**RAQIM** *hands the book back to* **RASHA**.)

RASHA. Yes. Yes, I see. Thank you.

RAQIM. I've been…helping. Fighting for Iraq in my own way. Without anyone knowing.

RASHA. Oh I've heard of such things. Tell me.

RAQIM. You have it right there in your hand.

RASHA. I don't understand.

RAQIM. I've been hiding books. The librarian of Basra has been hiding all the books from the library.

RASHA. The library's been looted and destroyed.

RAQIM. Yes, but we got many of the books out. They're hidden all over the city. I hid this book here thinking I was helping in my own small way. But then finally I found her and said, "I want to help in a larger way."

RASHA. *(laughs)* That's not what I thought you were going to tell me you'd done. Isn't it funny how people can read stories differently? Interpret them differently.

RAQIM. Yes. Yes, it is.

RASHA. I have to go. The curfew.

RAQIM. Do you like the end?

RASHA. No. I don't.

RAQIM. Didn't you read it?

(*He opens the book in her hands and points to the page.* **RASHA** *is taken aback by his physical proximity, but she is also fascinated by him. After a moment, she reads.* **DANIEL** *continues his presentation and the story unfolds.*)

DANIEL. "So Inana the sun goddess said to Lugalbanda that victory would come to the King if he promised to renew the city and settle it. Then all the riches of Arratta would be his.

(**MR. REKERS** *continues reading at home.*)

MR. REKERS. Now Aratta's battlements are covered in gold.

DANIEL. Its walls and its towering brickwork are bright red –

MR. REKERS. – their clay made of tinstone –

DANIEL & MR. REKERS. – dug out in the mountains where the cypress grows."

*(Lights fade on **DANIEL** and **MR. REKERS**.)*

RAQIM. How can't you like an ending like that? Peace. Renewal.

RASHA. Invasion and defeat.

RAQIM. Maybe enemies can restore each other in the end.

RASHA. I don't want to see all of Iraq flattened to the ground in the false hope that the Americans will rebuild us. They won't rebuild us. They'll leave us to rot with nothing to shield us from the wind and the heat. There will be no divine intervention for us. No ancient bird to swoop down and guide us to safety.

RAQIM. We're young. I won't give up on hope.

RASHA. We may be young, but this land, our home, is older than the story in this book. It's older than all of the stories, older than the stories of all other peoples put together. And we're part of it. Part of the dust we stand on. Can't you hear it? The rumbling in the earth. All of our ancestors. They're waking up. They can feel the footfalls of foreign boots overhead. They're calling for us to hold true to who we are. This is our land, for thousands of years. No one is going to occupy it but us.

*(**RASHA** hands the book back to **RAQIM**.)*

Thank you for your story. It's taught me many things.

*(She leaves. Lights up on **WINSTON** and **CYNTHIA** in the front of the class. They have just received their projects back with their grades on it. **CYNTHIA** raises her hand, waving.)*

CYNTHIA. Mrs. Litvinis...? Yeah, I see here that we all got B pluses, and I was just wondering if that had to do with the extension? I mean, would we have gotten an A if we didn't have to get that extension, because if we would've then I think that Winston and I should still get the A because we were prepared, and it isn't our fault that Daniel wasn't because he's just a screw up and we all know it, and everyone's always known it, ever since kindergarten when he got put in time out indefinitely for cutting off Caroline McMahon's ponytail, and so what did you expect? I mean come on, that is a C-plus average person if I ever saw one, and in reality he only got the B plus because of the work Winston and I did and I just think it's really, really, unfair that my chances to be accepted into an Ivy League school have probably just crashed into the basement because of –

> (**WINSTON** *puts the pith helmet on her head shutting her up just as the school bell rings. Lights down on them as lights come up on* **MR. REKERS** *at home, lost deep in thought.* **DANIEL** *enters. There is a bit of a pause and then he decides to speak.*)

DANIEL. Hey.

MR. REKERS. *(startled)* Oh. Hey there.

DANIEL. Didn't mean to scare you.

MR. REKERS. Nope. I was just – resting a bit. Sort of went away in my head and, well – …

> (*Pause as neither says anything.* **DANIEL** *heads for the stairs but then stops.*)

DANIEL. I do that too.

MR. REKERS. What?

DANIEL. Go away in my head. Like I'm in a place with someone, in the same room or right next to them even, just sitting or standing right there, and they think I'm ignoring them or hating them even, but I'm not. It's just that I'm some place else, like in my head, like tying to figure things out, you know?

MR. REKERS. Yeah. Yeah, I know.

(Pause again as neither says anything. **DANIEL** *heads for the stairs and stops again.)*

DANIEL. Dad?

MR. REKERS. UhHuh?

DANIEL. Your letters? Mom didn't take them. I did.

MR. REKERS. What?

DANIEL. One night – when I was like ten – you and mom were fighting, really going at each other, and you had been…you know, drinking alot, and she stormed out of the house and then you passed out and I – I was gonna leave. I was gonna run away. And I went into your room to get one of your duffle bags and I was tearing through the closet and…well, there they were, crammed in the back, stuffed into one of your combat boots.

(He takes a stack of letters stored in a plastic bagie out from his jacket and puts them on his fathers lap.)

I – I buried them in the backyard so – …well… I just wanted them to be mine.

MR. REKERS. They are yours. Have – have you read them?

DANIEL. Every single one. Do you wanna know my favorite?

MR. REKERS. Yeah. Yeah I would.

*(**DANIEL** takes out one of the letters and reads it to his father.)*

DANIEL. "Dear son – I have an apology to make. Sometimes I forget to think of you. There is such ugliness going on here that you slip my mind and I feel guilty because you always hear that during wartime, all a soldier can think about is home. And that *is* true most of the time. But sometimes I forget and all I can see and think of is the horror in front of me. But this morning, in the midst of it all, I heard crying. Crying is a frequent sound here, but this was different. This was not an Iraqi woman wailing over her dead son or a soldier writhing in pain. This was a new, but familiar sound.

And a memory stirred. Something woke up inside of me, like light shooting into a dark room."

(Lights up on **FAHAD** *reading a letter.)*

FAHAD. Dear Fahad – I'm leaving.

(Lights rise on **RAQIM** *composing the letter* **FAHAD** *is reading.)*

RAQIM & FAHAD. I can't stay here. I don't feel like I belong here anymore.

(Lights fade on **FAHAD**.*)*

RAQIM. We're citizens of Iraq. But who's going to lead us now? Sunnis? Shiites? The Americans? So I've decided it's time to lead myself. I am Iraqi yes, but as a citizen, well…? I think I'd like to try to be a citizen of the world. I'm going to Jerusalem. I want to see the Dome of the Rock and the Church of the Holy Sepulcher and the Wailing Wall. Can you imagine what a place it must be? Fighting, yes, and such division, but we're all there together, these three great faiths, side by side, whether we like it or not. Such faith. I want to see it. To feel it. And you and I? We'll see each other again. Let's make a pact my friend. That this coming Dul al-hijjah we'll meet in Mecca. We'll make the Hajj just as we always said we would. I think and dream of it often, of you and I in the Holy City hearing the first morning call to prayer.

(We hear the call to prayer as lights fade on **RAQIM** *as* **DANIEL** *continues reading his father's letter.)*

DANIEL. "I followed the sound – the crying. And it led me to a girl. Her hands were scraped. I guess she had been running along the road and fell."

(Lights up on **WINSTON** *in front of the class.)*

WINSTON. I read an article in the paper today about a suicide bombing in Basra, Iraq. The bomber was a sixteen year old girl. All that survived the blast was a stack of letters she had written, most of 'em destroyed.

But they printed the contents of one of them, and I thought I'd read it to you.

> (**DANIEL** *continues reading his father's letter. We see* **MR. REKERS** *young again re-enacting the moment talked about in the letter.*)

DANIEL. "I picked the little girl up off the road, and I handed her the Yoda keychain I gave to you when you were just a baby. I used to dangle it over your crib at night and you'd giggle away. I have always carried it with me over here for good luck. I handed it to her, and you know what Danny? Her crying stopped and she started to giggle just like you did. And then, I swung her round and round by her hands in a big circle and we laughed and laughed, and I thought of how you and I do that in our back yard at home, and it made me miss you all the more and love you all the more. I met her father and he's a good man. He wants peace for his country, for his family, just like we do. He tried to give the keychain back to me but I said –

DANIEL & MR. REKERS. 'No.'

MR. REKERS. 'No, it's a gift from my son to your daughter.' Just think Danny, you made a little Iraqi girl named Rasha laugh today from half way around the world without even knowing it."

> (**WINSTON** *reads from the newspaper to the class.*)

WINSTON. "My hated American enemy,"

> (*Lights rise on* **RASHA** *composing the letter* **WINSTON** *is reading.*)

WINSTON & RASHA. This is my last letter to you.

> (*Lights fade on* **WINSTON** *as* **RASHA** *continues.*)

RASHA. I don't know what to call this feeling toward you. I remember an American soldier swinging me around and around when I was a little girl, making me laugh. And he gave me a gift.

> (*She holds up the Yoda keychain.*)

That day gave me such a feeling. It was love I think. An American brought happiness and kindness and generosity to a little girl in Iraq. But not anymore. Now you only bring death, and hunger, and bombs, and fire, and hatred. There is such hatred here. They say it was always here but I feel that *you* have unleashed it into an even bigger fury: Sunni toward Shiite, Shiite toward Sunni, Iraqi toward American, American toward Iraqi. Why? Why do you hate us so much? So please tell me, what feeling am I to respond with? My love for you is gone. My happiness is gone. I can't call this new feeling hatred because it is beyond that. It is a feeling I cannot contain. It grows so big I feel like it's going to explode out of me. But I won't let you destroy me. No. I'll do it myself. I will be fire, and blood-soaked singed earth, and sirens, and screams. I will be terror. I will be this. I will do this. And I will take as many of you as I can with me. Your Iraqi…friend. Rasha

*(Lights fade on her as **DANIEL** continues reading his father's letter.)*

DANIEL. "I always end my letters. 'Love, Dad,' but you always have my love and always will. So tonight I will sign off with another word. 'Peace.' For, as your father, it is what I pray you will always have, until the end of days."

*(We hear the chant of the call to prayer as **DANIEL** folds the letter and puts it in his father's hand. **MR. REKERS** embraces his son as the lights fade.)*

End of Play

Civil Wars

CIVIL WARS was commissioned and produced in 2008 by Signature Theatre in Arlington, Virginia (Eric Schaeffer, Artistic Director, Maggie Boland, Managing Director) for their Signature in the Schools program (Marcia Gardner, Education Director). It was directed by Marcia Gardner, with scenic design by James Kronzer, costume design by Erin Nugent, lighting design by Mark Lanks, and sound design by Matt Rowe. The cast was as follows:

ALEK	Chris Stanton
JANE	Irene Casey
SAMUEL	Gary Kennedy
CELIA	Laura Razzuri
DOMENIC	John James Nell, Jr.
PRISCILLA	Kaye Siapno
ZAHARA	Safwa Saied
SYDNEY	Veronika Stumpo
CHAZ	April Archer
THALIA	Brenda Paula
DIANA	Ana Zamora
MRS. STITKOVIC	Sherri L. Edelen

CHARACTERS

MRS. STITKOVIC – Late 40s/Early 50s. A teacher at a private school in Northern Virginia. An immigrant from Bosnia. A fan of all things American.

ALEK – Mrs. Stitkovic's son at 18. He died during the Bosnian War. He is now a ghost and has come to haunt his mother.

JANE – 18. Named after Jane Fonda and is very proud of that fact. Very politically active in a very in your face way. Smart – maybe too smart for her own good.

SAMUEL – 18. A ghost. A black slave who is haunting the ground his family died on but which is now the ground of an elite girls' school. Passionate. A protector standing guard.

CELIA – 18. Latino. Number one in her class. She comes from a poor, violent, neighborhood and is at the school on a full scholarship. Both of her parents are dead. Her brother is in the military.

DOMENIC – 20. Latino. Celia's brother. In the army. He joined in order to be able to go to college when he is discharged. He is a fierce protector of his sister.

PRISCILLA – 18. A drama queen.

ZAHARA – 18. Has lived most of her life as a follower. Daughter of a diplomat. Was born in Darfur. Many of her family still lives there.

SYDNEY – 18. Very smart. Very involved but dissatisfied. Wishes to see the world. She has dual citizenship – US and Israeli.

CHAZ – 18. African American. Very bold. Doesn't fear anything. She hurtles through life with a ton of energy.

THALIA – 18. Tries to blend into the background. Longs for an easy life.

DIANA – 18. Seemingly meek. Does not want to cause trouble.

SETTING

A private girls' school in Virginia. 2007.

Scene 1
A Lacrosse Field. Afternoon.

*(We hear a snare drum keeping steady "battle time" as the lights fade to black. We sit in full darkness for a few short moments when suddenly there is an explosion of military brass – a rushing, pulsating, vigorous, triumphant, Sousa piece of music. Lights come up on two figures, one dressed as a Union soldier [**CELIA**], the other dressed as a Confederate soldier [**ZAHARA**]. Each is running at each other from opposite ends of the football field brandishing their respective sides' flag. They run around each other, the flags billowing. They circle the field fully and head toward each other using the flags as weapons. Five similarly dressed figures [**PRISCILLA, DIANA, THALIA** on the Union side, **SYDNEY** and **CHAZ** on the Confederate side], run on to the field brandishing rifles. The sides clash at center when suddenly one of the soldiers [**PRISCILLA**], rips her hat off and her hair comes tumbling down. All the other soldiers take off their caps revealing themselves to be girls as well.)*

PRISCILLA. Stop it, okay?! Just stop it! It's too hot okay? It's just – I mean it's really, really, hot and I just can't anymore, okay? I can't. I'm gonna faint. Do you want that? Do you want me to just collapse here of dehydration. DE – hydration. That's serious, okay? I could die. I could collapse here and die. And then you'd all have to deal with that, okay? So let's just stop. Jeez!

CHAZ. Oh, just shut it before I pound you.

DIANA. *(brandishing her gun)* No violence please. This is supposed to be fun!

PRISCILLA. Fun? ...Fun?! How is this remotely fun? I'm hot. I'm thirsty. I broke a nail, and I know that I just look really, really, bad!

(beat)

SYDNEY. Wow.

PRISCILLA. What?

SYDNEY. It's just your energy seems really, really negative right now.

PRISCILLA. Oh really?

SYDNEY. Yeah. Really. I can feel it.

PRISCILLA. Well, can you feel this?

(She flicks her forehead.)

CHAZ. No, you did not just do that.

ZAHARA. Uh uh. Not cool.

CELIA. Come on you guys, let's just all calm down.

CHAZ. Oh you can calm down, 'Cause you always get the good stuff.

ZAHARA. Yeah.

CHAZ. You get to carry a flag.

ZAHARA. A big flag.

CHAZ. You get to be on the Union side.

ZAHARA. Yeah.

CHAZ. Every year until now that's been me.

ZAHARA. Always.

CHAZ. That's been my flag.

ZAHARA. The big flag.

CHAZ. But this year you're brown-nosing the new teacher and suddenly I have to be a Confederate soldier.

ZAHARA. Both of us.

CHAZ. Suddenly.

ZAHARA. This year.

CHAZ. And look at us.

ZAHARA. Right here.

CHAZ. We're black.

ZAHARA. Both of us.

CHAZ. Black *Confederate* soldiers.

ZAHARA. What is that?

CHAZ. It's wrong, that's what it is, I mean really just wrong, and I don't want it anymore.

ZAHARA. Me either.

CHAZ. So I quit!

(She throws down her soldier's cap and gun.)

ZAHARA. Yeah.

(She throws hers down too.)

THALIA. *(picking up the caps)* Oh, you're gonna get them all dirty.

CHAZ. Who cares?! I'm sick of it.

(She takes the cap off of **THALIA**'s *head and throws it on the ground.)*

Every year making us do these Civil War re-enactments. I mean what are we learning and why am I out here in a costume acting out something for an American History class? We should be in a cool air-conditioned classroom somewhere reading stories about old stuff, not acting it out.

CELIA. Chaz –

CHAZ. Don't you talk to me! Miss Full Scholarship. Miss, "I get everything I want." Don't you even think of talking to me.

THALIA. Let's all calm down.

CHAZ. I don't want to be calm.

PRISCILLA. Shut up. It's too hot!

CHAZ. Cram it!

THALIA. We're supposed to be rehearsing!

CHAZ & PRISCILLA. Shut up!

THALIA. What did you say to me?!

(The following lines can all overlap.)

CHAZ. You heard me.

CELIA. Guys, please do not do this.

PRISCILLA. It's too hot.

DIANA. See? Violence. Violence!

SYDNEY. Okay, everybody! Quiet!!

(Everyone looks at her a little stunned.)

This is stupid. We don't have to act like freakin' animals, right? Can we all at least try to be civil?

PRISCILLA. What, are you like Miss Peace Keeper now?

SYDNEY. All I'm saying is, why don't we just take a vote? You know, like human beings.

CHAZ. A vote?

SYDNEY. Yes.

PRISCILLA. I don't get it.

SYDNEY. Voting. Like Democracy. Like peaceful resolution.

CHAZ. Oh please.

PRISCILLA. Ugh.

SYDNEY. Look, everyone who wants to continue rehearsing like we're supposed to, raise your hand.

*(**DIANA**, **SYDNEY**, and **THALIA** raise their hands.)*

Now everyone who wants to stop rehearsal for now and take a break, raise your hand.

*(**PRISCILLA**, **CHAZ**, and **ZAHARA** raise their hands.)*

PRISCILLA. Ooo, a tie, what a surprise.

SYDNEY. Okay. Who didn't vote?

CHAZ. Oh, I am just too tired.

(She sits down on the bleachers.)

SYDNEY. Come on, this is America guys. We're all supposed to vote.

(silence)

Guys!

(after a beat)

THALIA. It was Celia. *(to CELIA)* Sorry.

CHAZ. Hey. Keep your mouth shut. You don't go ratting on people.

ZAHARA. Uh uh. Not cool.

PRISCILLA. Oh please, you both hate her. What do you care?

CHAZ. Because you're not supposed to go around betraying people.

SYDNEY. Celia? Seriously? Of all people. How can number one in the class not vote?

CELIA. Look. I don't wanna get involved. You all decide.

SYDNEY. We can't. It's a tie. If you don't break the tie, we're stuck.

CHAZ. Hey look. I've decided. I'm not moving. I'm not rehearsing. Done. Over. Finished.

ZAHARA. Yeah.

CELIA. There you go.

(She sits down. All the other girls do also except for SYDNEY.)

SYDNEY. Well, isn't this just great?

CHAZ. Oh just sit down.

(From offstage we hear a Slavic voice through a bullhorn.)

MRS. STITKOVIC. *(offstage)* Hello? Hello?! ...Hello, you all, my dearest lovelies.

CHAZ. Oh God, here she comes.

MRS. STITKOVIC. *(offstage)* What are you all to doing? What is with all of this sitting! Up! Up! Up!

(MARTA STITKOVIC enters. She is dressed in full antebellum finery: hoopskirt, wide brimmed bonnet, and fan. She is yelling through a bullhorn.)

MRS. STITKOVIC. You cannot be with the sitting. There is work. Always the work. Always bettering. We can all do with the bettering.

DIANA. *(raising her hand)* Mrs. S?

MRS. STITKOVIC. *(still through the bullhorn)* Yes, Diana?

DIANA. Can you not talk through that thing?

MRS. STITKOVIC. *(through the bullhorn)* Oh!

(She turns the bullhorn off.)

Oh. Yes. I am sorry. I give to you apology. But what is with all of this? You all did promise to me that you would do the rehearsing until I was through with my last class and could get into my costume. It was to be big surprise.

(She twirls and poses.)

Do you like?

CHAZ. It's whack.

ZAHARA. It's crazy.

THALIA. *(quietly)* It's offensive.

MRS. STITKOVIC. Oh I know. I know my dearest lovelies. But it is the truth. The truth of what you come from. Here. Here in this land, this land of freedom, where so many have not been free. But this is the story. The story of you. So. I will speak. Before the re-enactment. Since I am an immigrant to this country I thought it will mean something that I shall do the speaking, talking of the freedoms, the price of the freedoms we all share and have. The spilt blood of brother from brother. We must all face the history, no? Yes. So.

(She grabs the bullhorn and shouts through it again.)

Pick up those rifles! Get into the positions! Formation, formation, formation!

(All the girls grumble as they pick up their rifles, put on their hats, and get into their positions.)

Move, move, move! We cannot afford this slowness. Fight the laziness my lovelies. Be better. Be better than you know yourself to be!!

(All the girls are back into positions: two armies facing each other. **MRS. STITKOVIC** *is on the bleachers now standing above the two opposing sides.)*

Wait. Wait. Do not move. Let the tension to be there. You must know to let it rise. To let the people watching hold their breath. Waiting. Wait... Wait... And... CHARGE!!!

(The girls run toward each other screaming.)

Wait!... Wait... STOP!!!!

CHAZ. Oh come on!

PRISCILLA. It's too hot!

*(**CHAZ** and **PRISCILLA** fall to the ground exhausted.)*

MRS. STITKOVIC. Where is Janie?!

CHAZ. Oh please...

MRS. STITKOVIC. Priscilla?!

PRISCILLA. De – Hy – Dra – Tion.

MRS. STITKOVIC. No, no, no! We have no time for the drama now. Strong, strong, strong! This is what we are to be, my little lovelies! Up, up, up!

(The girls get to their feet.)

(turning off bullhorn) Where is Janie? We cannot have this missing of rehearsal. She has missed too much. Too many. Why? Who knows this? Celia?

CELIA. I don't know Mrs. S.

MRS. STITKOVIC. We must all be in the planning and the rehearsing together. We cannot be alone in this. Otherwise we will all fall. So. Now. We tell her, no? We all talk to her and make her do what she has promised to do. So. *(back on the bullhorn)* Formation my little lovelies! Formation!!!

(The girls moan and grumble as they move into formation. As they do, we hear a loud whistle from offstage.)

PRISCILLA. Ok, this is just weird, what is going on?!

(JANE comes marching on to the field, dressed in jeans, a tie-dyed t-shirt with a huge peace sign on it, and a camouflage army jacket with many activist buttons (MIA, ERA, Pro Choice, Greenpeace) all over it. She has a silver referee whistle in her mouth and is carrying a large old boom box with stickers (Janis Joplin, Bob Marley, Jim Morrison, Joan Baez) all over it. She wears John Lennon style sunglasses. As she marches she toots on the whistle in a military like way, each blast matching her steps. She marches up the steps of the bleachers and sets the boom box down and turns it on. A song in the style of Lennon's "Give Peace A Chance*" fills the air. JANE walks back off and starts to carry on supplies: a tent, placards, signs, a deck chair, usurping the bleachers, setting up camp. Finally she hangs up a large banner stating, "Those Who Re-enact the Past are Doomed to Re-live it.")

MRS. STITKOVIC. What is this?

(JANE holds her hand out to her.)

JANE. May I?

(Dumbfounded, MRS. STITKOVIC hands the bullhorn to JANE.)

(politely to STITKOVIC) Thank you. *(through the bullhorn)* FRIENDS! CITIZENS! Are we going to stand for this?!

(Everyone looks at her confused.)

I say no! "Civil War Re-enactment." I say no to this glorification. I say no to paying homage to that pain, to that bloodshed, to that scar on our history. No, I say no! War. No! Peace. Yes!

---

*The publisher recommends that the licensee creates an original composition that stays true to the author's intent.

CHAZ. Whack.

MRS. STITKOVIC. What is this?

JANE. I'm protesting.

MRS. STITKOVIC. Protesting what?

JANE. This barbaric, antiquated, celebration of death, destruction, and the institution of slavery. I can't be a part of it.

> *(beat)*

MRS. STITKOVIC. Oh.

> *(The girls burst into laughter.)*

Hush! Hush now.

JANE. Why? As modern day citizens of Virginia, why are we celebrating this institution, this *Southern* institution of re-enacting a battle from a war – a *war* everybody – a war that divided this country, a divide that continues to rent us apart by the very act of us re-enacting these battles year after year.

PRISCILLA. Talk about drama.

JANE. And think about it. The South lost. And what were they fighting for? An institution that can, at best, be called abhorrent.

THALIA. Wow.

JANE. So we do what? March and wave flags and act out their pain, the pain and ugliness of war, the pain and ugliness of slavery. No more. No more. No more!

> *(She turns the bullhorn off and calmly gives it back to* **MRS. STITKOVIC.** *)*

Thank you.

> *(She sits down in her deck chair.* **MRS. STITKOVIC.** *goes over to* **JANE** *and kisses her on the forehead.)*

MRS. STITKOVIC. Brava! And magnifique.

> *(She speaks through the bullhorn.)*

See? See, my little lovelies. This is heart. This is why we teach.

*(She turns the bullhorn off and talks to **JANE**.)*

I am proud of you, why didn't you just tell me? You didn't have to skip the practices. You should have just turned and told me and I would have excused you.

PRISCILLA. Wait…

CHAZ. What?

JANE. No. no. I don't think you understand. It's not just about me. I'm going to stop you – this.

MRS. STITKOVIC. What?

JANE. This…tradition…has to stop. And I'm going to stop it.

*(**MRS. STITKOVIC** turns to the other girls.)*

MRS. STITKOVIC. That's it for today. Go. Go now!

THALIA. What's going on?

MRS. STITKOVIC. Nothing. Nothing. Keep going.

CHAZ. We shouldn't have to do it either.

ZAHARA. Yeah.

PRISCILLA. Yeah, why does Jane get out of it?

CHAZ. It's not fair.

ZAHARA. Not one bit.

MRS. STITKOVIC. You cannot jump on the bandwagon now, just because it brings the convenience.

PRISCILLA. But it's not fair. I – I believe in things too so –

MRS. STITKOVIC. No, no, it is too late to say these things now.

CHAZ. But what about freedom?

ZAHARA. Yeah, freedom.

CHAZ. Don't we have the right to say, "No, we don't want to do it?"

MRS. STITKOVIC. No, not now, I am the teacher. Go.

PRISCILLA. But –

MRS. STITKOVIC. Move, move, move!

CHAZ. Not cool.

*(The girls exit. **CELIA** lags behind.)*

CELIA. Mrs. S?

MRS. STITKOVIC. Not now dear.

CELIA. But I have to talk to you about next year.

MRS. STITKOVIC. Yes, yes, college, it is right that you are to be scared, but you must embrace the excitement of this thing, and such a school! Duke! And on full scholarship. I am so very proud. Such adventures you will to have.

CELIA. But –

MRS. STITKOVIC. Not now. Later in my office. Go, go go…

(CELIA leaves.)

So…my little Janie –

JANE. Please, I've been telling you all year, my name is Jane, not Janie.

MRS. STITKOVIC. Oh, it is only the pet expression of the caring I have to show for you.

JANE. Well, it's Jane. After Jane Fonda.

MRS. STITKOVIC. Oh! You never did tell me. I like her, that Jane Fonda. All those movies of hers – On the Golden Pond.

JANE. What?

MRS. STITKOVIC. Oh. Yes, I forget how young you are to be. You do not know of it maybe. A movie she did make with her father Henry. They played the father and she the daughter and they would always be at each other with the fighting. But in the end – they did realize how much they are to love each other. It did show me how the world should be. It did make me to cry. And I did like to watch those workout videos of hers. I try to lose the weight. Oh she was so slim. It made me to be jealous.

JANE. That was only after she had been sucked in by America's capitalistic, ego obsessed, vanity fueled, pop-culture machine. When she was young, she used to stand for things. She was a real rebel. That's who I was named after. Jane. See? Jane. Can you imagine people calling her Janie Fonda?

MRS. STITKOVIC. Well I am sure somebody did when she was just the little girl.

*(**DOMENIC**, dressed in a U.S. army uniform, enters on the fringes of the field and listens.)*

JANE. Look. It's a free country. I have the right to do this.

MRS. STITKOVIC. Yes, yes, my little lovely, but this is a private school.

JANE. So are you gonna turn me in? Shut me down?

MRS. STITKOVIC. I'm sure the rules of the school say something about –

JANE. You always say we have to be aware of history. I am.

MRS. STITKOVIC. Yes.

JANE. And not only that, but I'll be changing history, making history!

MRS. STITKOVIC. Yes… Yes! I will fight this. I will help you. I will talk to the administration. You should not be stopped.

*(She goes to **JANE**, grabs her face and kisses her on both cheeks.)*

I am off!

*(She heads off and runs into **DOMENIC**, startled.)*

Ah!

DOMENIC. Oh, I'm sorry. I'm sorry ma'am.

MRS. STITKOVIC. No, it is I who –

DOMENIC. I didn't mean to scare –

MRS. STITKOVIC. Oh, no, it's just that – I – … you… I was startled. Excuse me.

DOMENIC. Mrs. Stitkovic?

MRS. STITKOVIC. Yes, yes that's me. Do I –?

DOMENIC. I'm Celia Castillo's brother Domenic.

MRS. STITKOVIC. Oh! Oh, yes, yes!

DOMENIC. She talks about you a lot.

MRS. STITKOVIC. Oh...!

DOMENIC. She says she wishes you had been here all four years.

MRS. STITKOVIC. Oh. Oh...!

DOMENIC. She thinks you're a great teacher.

MRS. STITKOVIC. Oh, no, I am a student really here *(puts her hand over her heart)* and here *(points to her head)* just as she, just as all my girls. So teaching here at this school is just more of the learning for me. I do not stay in the one place very long. I have traveled the world, many countries in the past thirteen years, over twenty of them. But this country I spend the longest – two years. I have traveled this country of yours, learning of all the states, reading of all the history. And now I am here. Virginia. It is a great place you are able to do the defending of.

DOMENIC. Yes.

   (beat)

I just stopped by to see her.

MRS. STITKOVIC. Oh. Oh, she didn't say anything about –

DOMENIC. She doesn't know.

MRS. STITKOVIC. Oh.

DOMENIC. It's a surprise.

MRS. STITKOVIC. Oh!

DOMENIC. Do you know where I might find her?

MRS. STITKOVIC. Well, she was just here rehearsing. We could go find her together if you'd like.

DOMENIC. Well, I'd like to see her privately ma'am. There're some things I need to talk to her about alone. Can I just wait for her in her room?

MRS. STITKOVIC. Oh, no, no, no, boys are not allowed in the dorms, even family.

DOMENIC. Ah.

MRS. STITKOVIC. I tell you. Why do I not go to find her and bring her here to you?

DOMENIC. Oh no…

MRS. STITKOVIC. Yes, yes, it would be the pleasure for me to do this for you.

DOMENIC. Thank you ma'am. That's very kind of you.

MRS. STITKOVIC. Well…family. It is of the most importance. So… I will do this.

*(She exits leaving the bullhorn behind. Pause as **JANE** just stares at **DOMENIC**.)*

DOMENIC. Hi.

JANE. I didn't know Celia had a brother.

DOMENIC. Oh. Well, here I am.

JANE. She's never said anything.

DOMENIC. Are you two good friends.

JANE. Well… I mean, we know each other. We take a lot of the same classes. We're like co-number ones.

DOMENIC. Jane?

JANE. Umm…yeah.

DOMENIC. She talks a lot about school.

JANE. Oh.

DOMENIC. She likes it here.

JANE. Well, like I said, she hasn't ever said a thing about you.

(pause)

DOMENIC. *(pointing out her "camp")* That's quite a set up.

JANE. Yeah.

*(Silence as **JANE** just stares at **DOMENIC**. He looks around taking in the field.)*

DOMENIC. Amazing field you guys got. My high school didn't have anything like this.

JANE. The school has a lot of rich alumni.

DOMENIC. Lucky.

JANE. Yeah.

*(Another long silence as **JANE** stares at **DOMENIC**.)*

DOMENIC. So...

JANE. Just so you know, I don't believe in death.

DOMENIC. Uhh... I don't think you're alone there.

JANE. What about you?

DOMENIC. Death is not at the top of the list of things I believe in. Pretty sure it's going to happen at some point to all of us, but I'm not cheering for it.

JANE. Oh yeah?

DOMENIC. Yeah. So...where you planning on going to school next –

JANE. *(grabbing the bullhorn and shouting through it)* War is death!! War is death!! War is death!! War is death!! *(repeat as needed)*

>   *(**DOMENIC** looks around startled not sure of what to do.)*

DOMENIC. Ok, umm...so...yeah...umm...can you –? Yeah, maybe I should just –

>   *(**MRS. STITKOVIC** comes running on to the field with **CELIA** right behind her.)*

MRS. STITKOVIC. What is happening here?! What is –?! Janie? ...Janie...? Jane!!

>   *(She grabs the bullhorn from **JANE**, and **JANE** stops her shouting.)*

This is – ...It is outrage! You say you want to do the protesting. That is your right, yes. Civil disobedience as you call it here in this country. But what you are doing here, now, in front of a guest, the brother of a classmate, this is not *civil* to me. Come.

>   *(**JANE** sits.)*

Be smart my little lovely. I offered to give you the help, to talk to the administration, and now you go and do this, to make it harder for me.

JANE. I didn't ask you to do that –

MRS. STITKOVIC. You –

JANE. I simply asked if you were going to shut me down. I didn't ask for help. You offered it, so you can't lay that on me.

MRS. STITKOVIC. Ah, she is like the politics. Talk what makes her to look good. This is full of the foolishness. Stand up.

> (**JANE** *doesn't budge.*)

Do not go to war with me young lady. I know war. You know it from the t.v. and the movies only, but I have seen it up close, so I will win.

JANE. I'll take my chances.

MRS. STITKOVIC. And we wonder why the civilizations topple to the ground, why dictators are hanged by their ankles in the square of the city. The stubbornness. It is good, yes to have the belief, but when you do not listen to others, you are to be left all alone, with no one to help to protect you. Allies, my little lovely. You will need them. So. If you sit here, unwilling to talk civilly, unwilling to accept others help, I will not come to your aid. But. If you decide, now, to take responsibility for the statement you want to make, for the battle you want to wage, and if you come with me and go to the administration, yourself, to talk, to negotiate, to come to terms with them, on how this protest of yours is the perfect example of how we are to teach our little lovelies of the greater world around them, if you are to do this, then I will sit beside you there, in that place, and I will offer you my support.

> (*She holds out her hand to* **JANE**.)

Come.

> (*Beat.* **JANE** *stands up and begins walking, passing by* **MRS. STITKOVIC**, *who follows.* **DOMENIC** *and* **CELIA** *stare after them. Once they are gone, they burst into laughter.*)

DOMENIC. Whoa.

CELIA. Crazy, right?

(She runs and gives him a bear hug.)

What are you doing here? I thought you headed back overseas yesterday.

(He pulls a letter out from his pocket.)

DOMENIC. No, day after tomorrow, and thank God 'Cause I couldn't just let this go without seeing you face to face to make sure you haven't gone crazy on me.

(**CELIA** *just stares at the letter.*)

CELIA. Oh.

DOMENIC. Mom and Dad are rolling over in their graves.

CELIA. I think they'd be proud.

DOMENIC. Explain this to me now.

CELIA. Don't flip out.

DOMENIC. Too late.

CELIA. I'm doing this, so let's just end the conversation now.

DOMENIC. You are not joining the army!

CELIA. How many times did I say that to you? And you didn't listen.

DOMENIC. You don't *have* to go. I did.

CELIA. Nobody *has* to go.

DOMENIC. Look. You got a free ride to this school. You got a full scholarship to college. It's what we dreamed about since we were kids. Now stop being an idiot.

CELIA. You're doing something important. Fighting for something important.

DOMENIC. What?

CELIA. None of my friends here even know about you. 'Cause if they did, then I'd have to tell them about you being over there, and most of 'em think like their parents. "The war is so bad. The war was such a mistake." And they may say that they support you, but really, they just think you're over there torturing men and raping little girls. And so if they knew, they'd be like, all caring and concerned to my face but really they think it's wrong. They think you're wrong for going or just stupid for going. But I don't. I think you're brave for going. I think it's right we're over there. So I wanna go too.

DOMENIC. When did your brain like shrivel up?

CELIA. What?

DOMENIC. I'm there for one reason – so I can go to school when I get out. You already got what most of us over there want, so stop being selfish and get to some class or some library and start learning something.

CELIA. Selfish?

DOMENIC. Yeah. I'd kill to have what you have. It's crazy what you're talking about. You have no idea what it's like over there, and you're talking all this romantic, patriotic, rah rah stuff.

CELIA. Look, there's such a thing as like safety in the world.

DOMENIC. Oh, jeez, you think it's safe over –

CELIA. Fighting for safety. I have never ever, felt safe. But when I look at the news and I see all of you over there, fighting for us, I do.

DOMENIC. Well guess what Sis? It's not because of Operation Iraqi Freedom or troop surges or the freakin' Patriot Act. You feel safe 'cause you aren't in a war zone anymore.

CELIA. What are you talking about?

DOMENIC. Oh, Mom and Dad killed in a drive-by when you were six, just sitting on our front porch while you played with a doll at their feet and you crying like crazy when I took it from you even though it was covered in their blood. And you wonder why you don't feel safe in this country? It's not us over there fighting someone else's war that makes you feel better. It's 'cause you're outta there, outta that bombed out neighborhood that looks a lot like some streets in Baghdad I've seen.

CELIA. You're getting off the subject.

DOMENIC. No, this is the subject!

CELIA. No it's –

DOMENIC. It's not our war –

CELIA. Yes, it –

DOMENIC. – and it never was, but we're paying for it!

CELIA. You're starting to sound like all –

DOMENIC. I went over there so my President could have a pissing contest for oil, and now I'm trying to stay alive while Sunnis and Shiites destroy their own country killing each other in a freakin' civil war –

CELIA. It's not really a –

DOMENIC. It is. The reporters and politicians can argue about it all they want, but that's what it is. And then on leave I get to come home and watch gangs tearing up my own neighborhood doing the same thing. My whole life is a war zone.

CELIA. What are you –

DOMENIC. And you sit here in your ivory tower of a private school talking about feeling unsafe.

CELIA. Look I didn't ask to be sent here. I can't help it that I'm smart.

DOMENIC. No you can't, so start acting like you are.

CELIA. I thought you wanted me to come here.

DOMENIC. I did. I do. Stay here! Go to college! Be one of the people who doesn't have to do the fighting. If you're rich or you're smart you don't have to get stuck killing rival gang members in your own neighborhood here at home or get shipped off to kill people even poorer than you are in some god-forsaken country halfway around the world.

CELIA. Dom please –

DOMENIC. Listen to me. If you do this thing, if you join up, I'll do something that throws me into a military prison for the rest of my life, and you'll have to live with the fact that you caused it.

CELIA. You wouldn't.

DOMENIC. You know me. I'll do it. I swear to you. If I even hear of you talking about this idea again I'll –

CELIA. Fine… Fine.

(long pause)

DOMENIC. I should get going.

CELIA. Yeah.

DOMENIC. Ok.

(A moment. Will they hug goodbye? They don't.)

CELIA. Be careful.

DOMENIC. Always am.

(He leaves. We hears the crowd of girls voices from offstage. **CELIA** *hides next to the bleachers not wanting to be seen.)*

PRISCILLA. *(offstage)* You are so lying.

JANE. *(offstage)* I'm telling you, they said yes.

SYDNEY. *(offstage)* Wow.

*(***JANE*** *heads onto the bleachers followed by* ***PRISCILLA, SYDNEY, CHAZ, ZAHARA, THALIA,*** *and* ***DIANA.****)*

CHAZ. You're doing this for extra credit, aren't you?

JANE. Oh please.

THALIA. Are you going to stay out here all night?

JANE. I'm going to stay out here as long as it takes.

SYDNEY. Wow.

DIANA. Creepy.

CHAZ. Whack.

JANE. Look. This is a big deal guys. This is important. This land that we're sitting on, that we play games on… death has occurred. Hallowed ground. That's what we're standing on.

PRISCILLA. Eeww.

CHAZ. Cool.

JANE. People died. Right here. In a war. Brother killing brother. And we are celebrating it. Holding it up like some great thing. Reliving it in front of an audience so people can like watch. Right here.

SYDNEY. Actually Jane, not really.

JANE. Excuse me?

SYDNEY. The battle we're re-enacting took place like ten miles from here.

THALIA. What?

PRISCILLA. Wait.

DIANA. I don't get it.

SYDNEY. I mean, did you really think it happened on this exact spot? And if such a famous battle had happened on this exact spot, do you think they would have built some fancy girls' school on top of it?

CHAZ. *(to* **JANE***)* Bet Harvard ain't too psyched they picked you right about now.

PRISCILLA. Okay. So let me get this straight. We're re-enacting something that didn't even happen here. We're like sweating in the sun, dressed like guys for something that is like a false history?

CHAZ. Oh, I think I need to hit someone.

DIANA. No violence please.

THALIA. It's a class guys. It's for a class. A history class. It doesn't have to be like real. It's history.

JANE. Exactly.

SYDNEY. What?

JANE. The fact is the Civil War happened. Wars happen. Battles are fought and blood is spilt. And it doesn't matter where it was spilt 'Cause the fact is, it was, no matter where you are, so you might as well fight against it wherever you are, even if you're in the wrong place.

(Silence as no one really understands a word she just said.)

PRISCILLA. Wouldn't you think a history teacher would like, know that? Would like, know that we're in the wrong place?

THALIA. She can barely speak English, why would she know something like that?

CHAZ. Because she's a teacher.

ZAHARA. Yeah.

CHAZ. I'm telling you, that Stitkovic, there's something wrong there.

ZAHARA. So wrong.

DIANA. I like her.

PRISCILLA. You like everybody.

CHAZ. I just want to stomp her sometimes with that accent.

ZAHARA. Yeah, what's with the accent?

DIANA. Violence, no violence.

SYDNEY. Guys, Morrisson made us do the same thing before she retired so you can't blame it on Mrs. S.

PRISCILLA. Where is she from anyway? Like Russia? Isn't she like communist of something?

JANE. Russia isn't communist anymore.

CHAZ. And Harvard breathes a sigh of relief.

SYDNEY. She's from Bosnia.

PRISCILLA. Where-ia?

THALIA. Oh! They like worship trees right?

JANE. What?!

THALIA. You know like standing in a circle, holding hands, around a tree.

PRISCILLA. Like in the Grinch?

THALIA. No. Like praying to the tree. Tree worshippers.

JANE. What are you talking about?

SYDNEY. Those? Are Druids.

THALIA. Oh.

JANE. I can't take anymore.

(She goes and sits in her deck chair and puts on headphones.)

CHAZ. Letting Jane off the hook like that but still making us do it, that's not right I'm sorry, it just isn't, so why does she get to speak too?

THALIA. Who?

CHAZ. Stitkovic.

ZAHARA. Yeah.

CHAZ. She's not even from here, so why does she get to speak about freedom before the re-enactment?

ZAHARA. Yeah.

SYDNEY. And why don't you start speaking for yourself?

THALIA. Ooo…

(Silence as everyone just waits to see what's going to happen.)

DIANA. Calm. Calm.

CHAZ. What did you say?

SYDNEY. I was talking to Zahara. She can speak for herself, can't she? Or does she just follow you around agreeing with everything you say?

DIANA. No violence please.

SYDNEY. *(to ZAHARA)* And why don't you speak for yourself? Your father's a diplomat for pete's sake. You've traveled the world.

THALIA. Wait.

CHAZ. Diplomat?

SYDNEY. But you walk behind her like a little puppy dog with no fight, no backbone. You think your family would like you acting like that, with all they're going through back in –

CHAZ. What is she talking –

ZAHARA. *(changing the subject)* She's Muslim!

CHAZ. What?

SYDNEY. Zahara!

ZAHARA. Stikovic. She's Muslim.

PRISCILLA. She is soooo not Muslim.

DIANA. She can't be.

THALIA. I don't get it.

PRISCILLA. She's white. With like an accent that's like not a Muslim accent.

SYDNEY. A Muslim accent?

PRISCILLA. Oh, you know what I mean.

SYDNEY. No actually I don't. Do you Zahara?

ZAHARA. Shut it.

SYDNEY. What do you all think the Bosnian War was about?

CHAZ. I honestly have no idea.

PRISCILLA. Who cares? Jeez! Why don't you go and like, pitch a tent with Jane or run off and find Celia? The three of you can sit around and read stuff to each other and get smarter and leave us alone so we can have a real life.

SYDNEY. Look –

ZAHARA. Ethnic cleansing.

(pause as they all look at her)

The Bosnian War. That's what it was about.

THALIA. Whoa.

SYDNEY. Well, yes, of course. But it's a little more complicated than that? It was a civil war not just –

PRISCILLA. What are they doing letting Muslims like her in the country?

SYDNEY. This was over ten years ago? Does no one listen in history class? She was probably running for her life if she's Muslim. And just because she's Bosnian doesn't mean she's –

CHAZ. She's not from here.

PRISCILLA. Exactly. And she's teaching us like, *American* History. American History. She's not an American so why is she teaching us about America?

CHAZ. Exactly.

PRISCILLA. And I mean, maybe she is a communist. I mean she could have been back when there were communists 'Cause she really does sound Russian to me so maybe she still is.

SYDNEY. She's Bosnian.

CHAZ. How do you know?

SYDNEY. I asked!

PRISCILLA. She sounds Russian.

THALIA. She does.

SYDNEY. The Slavic languages. There are similarities, so –

CHAZ. Why do you know so much?

ZAHARA. Yeah.

THALIA. Wait. Are we talking like a terrorist Muslim, or what?

CHAZ. Exactly.

ZAHARA. Hello!

SYDNEY. Oh, don't even –

CHAZ. It could happen.

ZAHARA. Hello!

DIANA. Wow.

SYDNEY. This is ridiculous.

*(She goes to exit and walks by **CELIA** hiding, startling herself.)*

Jeez. What are you doing hiding?

CHAZ. Probably spying for Stitkovic. Teacher's pet.

CELIA. I was just sitting here.

PRISCILLA. You're always just sitting somewhere. Always alone. I don't like it. It's starting to creep me out.

CHAZ. Yeah…

ZAHARA. Yeah.

*(**SYDNEY** just looks at **ZAHARA**.)*

SYDNEY. I'm out of here.

ZAHARA. Good.

*(She leaves. The other girls start to walk down and encircle **CELIA**. **JANE** takes notice and takes off her headphones, stands, and listens.)*

PRISCILLA. Miss Perfect. Always quiet. Why are you always so quiet?

CHAZ. Yeah.

ZAHARA. Yeah.

THALIA. You are quiet.

DIANA. Violence. Is this going to get violent?

PRISCILLA. What are you hiding?

THALIA. Yeah.

CHAZ. Must be hiding something.

ZAHARA. Always hiding something.

JANE. She had a visitor.

>   *(pause)*

CHAZ. What?

JANE. A guy.

PRISCILLA. Really? A boy for Celia on campus. Where is he now?

CHAZ. Yeah.

THALIA. Celia's got a boyfriend…

CHAZ. Tell us.

ZAHARA. Yeah.

PRISCILLA. Come on tell us.

DIANA. Violence. Violence!

>   *(They circle **CELIA**, taunting her with "Come on," "Tell us," "Celia has a boyfriend." Until finally:)*

JANE. Stop it!

>   *(Everything stops.)*

It was just one of those money guys from Duke, checking up, saying hi, making sure her grades are still okay.

CHAZ. That's it?

PRISCILLA. Jane? Why do you have to be so…like you are?

>   *(All the girls exit, leaving **JANE** and **CELIA** alone. The two girls just look at each other. **CELIA** leaves. **JANE** sits in her deck chair and puts her headphones back on.)*
>
>   *(Lights fade.)*

Scene 2
The Bleachers. Dusk

(JANE *is asleep in her deck chair.* SAMUEL *appears. He goes up to her and taps her on the knee. She awakens with a start.*)

JANE. Ah!

SAMUEL. What you doing?

JANE. What? – I'm… What? – Who – I'm –

SAMUEL. I can see what you're trying to do.

JANE. Boys – Boys aren't allowed on campus. Especially at night so…

SAMUEL. Ain't night yet.

JANE. Well, it's gonna be soon, so I have to ask you to leave.

SAMUEL. You shouldn't be doing it. You ain't got no right.

JANE. I have a whistle. See?

(*She pulls the silver whistle out of her pocket and holds it up.*)

I don't want any trouble. But I'll blow it. I will. And people will run out. The dorms? They're right over there. You won't get away if you do something.

SAMUEL. You don't know what you're talking about. Your signs. All your talking. You don't know nothing.

JANE. Hey. I have a 4.0 grade point average.

SAMUEL. What?

JANE. I'm practically number one in my class, well tied really if you ask me, but they don't do co-number ones here, so they averaged in all four years to decide, and just because Celia got an A in Trig junior year and I just got a B+, I wind up as number two. But I had mono, okay? Mono! I could barely sit up in bed, but I did all my work. I read *A Passage to India* for crying out loud. Glands swollen, high fever, but still I read it. And I came back to school weeks earlier than I should have, but I did it. 'Cause I care. I care about my education.

That should count for something. But no one seems to take that into account, so here I sit at number two, and so Celia will get to give the speech at graduation, and I have a great speech. I've been writing it since the seventh grade, but no one's gonna get to hear it now. Still, Celia's going to Duke. I'm going to Harvard next year. So there.

SAMUEL. *(with a sarcastic laugh)* Figures.

JANE. What's that supposed to mean?

SAMUEL. Heading North.

JANE. Well, yeah. That's where Har –

SAMUEL. Was you born here?

JANE. What?

SAMUEL. Virginia. Was you born in Virginia?

JANE. Yes.

SAMUEL. *(laughing)* Sitting here fighting for land that you can't wait to get away from.

JANE. What are you talking a –

SAMUEL. Running away from it 'cause you can smell it – the sweat in the fields. People think that smell goes away. But it don't. Even after a hundred and fifty years 'cause it's deep down in the earth, baked dry by a hot Southern sun, and then the rains dredge it up, that smell of sweat mixed with the blood and the tears. That's a certain kind of smell. That don't go away.

JANE. *(a little stunned by him)* No. *(getting excited)* No it doesn't.

(She starts rummaging through her backpack.)

Look. Do you mind if I write that down? 'Cause that's good. That is really good.

SAMUEL. You can't run from it.

JANE. *(desperately trying to find something to write with)* Wait, wait, just hold that thought please, 'cause I really want to get this down.

SAMUEL. You're gonna go North and get all uppity, trying to forget where you come from, *what* you come from, what your past is, but it ain't no better up there 'cause *they* ain't no better. They think they won something, some moral victory, but they weren't no better. They weren't fighting for us neither. They didn't go to war to get me outta chains.

JANE. *(confused)* Wait... What?

SAMUEL. You think those Union soldiers who fought on this land cared about me? Cared if I was free? They cared about their selves. They weren't fighting for me. They were fighting for America, for what they thought America should be, and that didn't include me. Me being free was just an afterthought as far as I can see. You all didn't go to War to fight over us. You went to War to fight for yourselves. For *your* rights. And we supposed to be thankful for that?

JANE. *(awed, stunned, scared)* Who are you?

(beat)

SAMUEL. Name's Samuel.

*(**SYDNEY** appears. **SAMUEL** doesn't move and sits right next to **JANE**. **SYDNEY** can't see **SAMUEL**.)*

SYDNEY. Hey.

JANE. *(totally startled and completely freaked out)* Aaaahhhhh!

SYDNEY. Whoa. Chill.

JANE. Ummm...

SYDNEY. Think you'd seen a ghost or something.

JANE. Umm...

SYDNEY. Hey, I don't blame you. I'd be totally freaked sitting out here all alone. Don't you get scared?

JANE. Oh, no, no, no, I'm fine.

SYDNEY. I thought I heard you talking to yourself as I was walking up.

JANE. Oh, I was. Just practicing a speech you know?

SYDNEY. Well good, 'cause I can't have you going crazy on me. Can I talk to you about something?

(SAMUEL starts making ghostly noises. SYDNEY doesn't hear them of course, but JANE does.)

JANE. *(trying to get her out of there)* Sydney, I really have to finish this speech so…

SYDNEY. I *really* admire what you're doing. I mean really.

JANE. Thanks Syd, but –

SYDNEY. I mean, fighting for what you believe in –

JANE. Can we talk about this tomorr –

SYDNEY. I feel like such a fraud.

JANE. You are so not a –

SYDNEY. I'm Israeli.

(SAMUEL's ghostly sounds stop. Silence.)

SAMUEL. What?

JANE. Wait –

SYDNEY. Just let me get this out. I was born there okay? I have dual citizenship, okay? But I haven't been there in a really, really, long time, but suddenly my parents are like, "You should go and join the Army over there."

JANE. Wait – What?

SYDNEY. It's like the law over there for kids our age. You have to join the army. And so my parents are all like, "You're Israeli. It's your duty. You should go."

JANE. Whoa.

SYDNEY. Yeah, and I'm like, "When did we become like Zionists?" And they're like, "You're denying your heritage." And I'm like, "No." But I mean, I just can't. I mean, I don't know. I don't know what that is. Over there. I mean, all that fighting. And bombing. Like suicide bombings. And children. Children throwing rocks at tanks. People dying at like, Sbarro.

JANE. Wait. What?

SYDNEY. Sbarro.

JANE. Like the pizza?

SYDNEY. Yeah, like sitting there just eating, and then… Boom. But still it's not like a war, right? It's just terrorism, right? Both sides saying the other are terrorists. And like on the news they just call it a crisis – "The Mid East Crisis" or "Crisis in the Middle East." But a crisis seems kinda little to me, but if bombs are going off and people are dying and calling each other terrorists, and fighting over land, well, that sounds like war to me, but its not, really, by definition I mean so – ?

JANE. You don't have to go.

SYDNEY. I know. But should I?

JANE. I – ...I don't know Syd.

SYDNEY. Come on, you're the smart one.

JANE. Not so smart today.

SYDNEY. Yeah, I'm sorry about that. Me blowing off my big mouth.

JANE. You should be going to Harvard instead of me.

SYDNEY. No thank you. I'm going to enjoy taking a year off. Unless I go into the Israeli army. Oh my God! Jane, you gotta help me out with this, and I don't get it. I mean, how can I go fight for something that I just don't get?

JANE. You're really Israeli?

SYDNEY. Well, half – I mean dual citizenship, that's what I said right? Right? But – See? See, this is why I don't tell anyone. Because you're gonna be like, "You're why everyone hates us. This is why the Arabs hate us. This is why there's terrorism. Why don't you just let the Palestinians have their own state?" But I don't live there okay, I don't, so you can say all you –

JANE. No, no, Syd, no. I don't care. I think it's cool. I mean, come on. It's cool.

SYDNEY. Yeah?

JANE. Yeah. It's just – I've known you for a long time, right? I mean we've been friends for a long time, so why don't I know this about you? Why don't I know anything about anyone I know?

SYDNEY. Everyone's afraid I guess.

> *(She gets up to leave.)*

Except you. You're brave. I'm terrified.

> *(She leaves.)*

SAMUEL. That girl is smart.

JANE. Yes, she is.

SAMUEL. She knows not to fight for something she don't understand, that don't have nothing to do with her.

JANE. Some people fight for what they believe in. I am. And those Union soldiers fought for you no matter what you say, no matter whether they thought they were or cared if they were. In the end their fighting was for you.

SAMUEL. Then why don't you just leave and go up North?

JANE. What are you doing here? What do you want from me.

SAMUEL. My brother lies here. My mother. Buried in the dirt she was raped on by the white man who owned her. They's here. They died on this land. So did I. I been watching over it, taking care of it, before any of your marching, and flags, and music ever thought to be here. Laying flowers, saying prayers, watching over. You don't know that. You don't care about that. You think you're fighting for me, but you ain't, and I didn't ask you to, so don't.

JANE. I got a right to be here.

SAMUEL. So do I.

JANE. I can't argue with that.

> *(SAMUEL goes to the top of the bleachers and sits on the top step.)*

SAMUEL. I ain't leaving.

> *(JANE lies back down in her lawn chair, puts the whistle around her neck, and lays one hand over it as she closes her eyes.)*

JANE. Neither am I.

> *(Lights fade.)*

Scene 3
The Bleachers. Night

(MRS. STITKOVICH enters onto the bleachers. SAMUEL still sits unseen. She is wearing a long cardigan sweater and is carrying, a blanket, a book, a flashlight, and a large container of coffee. She takes the blanket and puts it over JANE.)

MRS. STITKOVIC. *(whispering)* I here to watch over. Someone must always be to watch over. In case.

(She climbs up the bleachers, pours herself a cup of coffee, opens the book, and uses the flashlight to help her read. She sits reading in silence for a few moments when we hear the feint strains of a Bosnian folk tune. She shoots the flashlight beam out into the dark.)

(whispering) Hello?

(Silence. She goes back to her reading. We hear the tune again but this time whistled [it should be recorded.] She aims the flashlight on JANE's face. She is still asleep.)

(whispering) Jane?

(silence)

It is just the dark playing the tricks on the mind and ears.

(Silence as she tries to go back to her reading. The music starts again, and she shoots the beam out again and begins walking over the bleachers, searching for the source of the sound, and she begins humming along with the tune. The recorded whistling joins in. Then we hear a voice out of the darkness.)

ALEK. Mother.

(She quickly shoots the beam across the space and it lands on the face of ALEK.)

MRS. STITKOVIC. No…

> (**ALEK** *whistles the folk tune.*)

MRS. STITKOVIC. It is… It cannot…

> (**ALEK** *continues whistling as he walks down the bleachers toward* **MRS. STITKOVIC**. *He stands right in front of her. She places her hands over his face, not quite believing he is real.*)

I know this. I know this face.

ALEK. Mother.

MRS. STITKOVIC. Alek? My Alek?

> (*She hugs him ferociously. The hug ends. He looks at her.*)

ALEK. (*matter of factly*) I go now.

> (*He heads up the bleachers. Stunned, she follows.*)

MRS. STITKOVIC. Wait… What? I – I don't –

ALEK. I am dead.

MRS. STITKOVIC. Yes, yes, but –

ALEK. So this is just a visitation. It cannot be to last.

MRS. STITKOVIC. But you are real. I touched you. You are here.

ALEK. If I were real and not just the visitation, would we not speak in our native tongue instead of the broken English?

MRS. STITKOVIC. What?

ALEK. I do the joke with you.

> (*Pause. She starts to laugh. It builds to a big laugh. Then she remembers* **JANE**'s *sleeping presence.*)

Do not stop to worry. She will not wake. I will not allow it. It is what I choose for here and now. She will not wake.

MRS. STITKOVIC. Is this a dream for me?

ALEK. No. We are allowed the visitation if we do choose.

MRS. STITKOVIC. We?

ALEK. Oh, yes, there are many, always at any place where the dead have been laid. There are many here right now. Much death has been here.

(**MRS. STITKOVIC** *looks around frightened.*)

Boo!

(**MRS. STITKOVIC** *screams.*)

ALEK. You were always easy to make the fear of.

MRS. STITKOVIC. What are you doing here?

ALEK. I would ask of you the same.

MRS. STITKOVIC. What? Oh, I did not want her to be out at night alone. You never know who –

ALEK. No, what are you doing in this country on this land away from your own?

MRS. STITKOVIC. I have been away a long time.

ALEK. Many years. Many places.

MRS. STITKOVIC. Yes. But I think I stay here. It is my home now. It is good here.

ALEK. But you did leave your home, your home that I did die for.

MRS. STITKOVIC. No… No… I did not leave you.

ALEK. But you *did* leave me there.

MRS. STITKOVIC. No…

ALEK. I did waste this.

MRS. STITKOVIC. What?

ALEK. This visit to you. I did waste it.

MRS. STITKOVIC. No… no…

ALEK. It is the places that are haunted. Not the people. Only the living can allow their memories to haunt them. This is not a memory. But we can choose to come and visit if we want hard enough. So… I did want. But you do the traveling. For years. I search for you. It is not easy, whatever you think about the ghostly powers. I did have to search because you never did stand still, never did stay in one place for very long. But finally, here I am. And now? I do regret it. So I go.

MRS. STITKOVIC. No, I want more time.

ALEK. We are too different.

MRS. STITKOVIC. No, no, we are of the same blood.

ALEK. My blood did spill for our people. You did run.

MRS. STITKOVIC. No, no, I did not run. I did choose to leave. I could not stay there, where they would give so much land back to them, to Serbians, who did destroy our land and kill my son. I could not stay there. Why should they have so much when we did lose so much more? Where in that is there justice?

ALEK. Sarajevo stands. And yet you wander this country reading books, and eating the food, trying to be an American.

MRS. STITKOVIC. No...

ALEK. I have been watching. I did see you this morning. You do not even wear the right dress. You wear the dress you see in the movies you would watch late at night on the videotapes when I was just a boy.

MRS. STITKOVIC. You have been here and saying nothing to me til now?

ALEK. It is the wrong dress from the *Gone With the Wind*. You wear the dress from before the war and you do not even know that it is wrong. And how do you teach the history to the children when you know nothing of it yourself?

MRS. STITKOVIC. I read, I do. I learn.

ALEK. You know nothing.

MRS. STITKOVIC. Alek! I am still your mother. Do not speak to me in that –

ALEK. They learn nothing from you.

MRS. STITKOVIC. I was a teacher back home. I was a great teacher.

ALEK. Because you knew of what you spoke. You cannot come here and teach them of themselves. You should teach them of yourself. But no. You travel the world, but you do not stay anywhere long enough to really learn anything of the place or the people. Not really. And you do not teach them of yourself, make them know of what you come from, so they learn nothing of you, and you learn nothing of them, and this is the way the world lives, knowing nothing of each other. And the people wonder why the earth is overrun with wars.

MRS. STITKOVIC. Alek, I –

(ALEK starts whistling the folk tune. He begins walking up the bleachers.)

MRS. STITKOVIC. You will not leave here! This is my memory now. You, here, are my memory now, so I will have it haunt me. And you will not leave.

(ALEK sits on the top of the bleachers the opposite end as SAMUEL. MRS. STITKOVIC sits back with her book and turns the flashlight on.)

I am reading of General Custard and how the Natives of this land did kill him only to be slaughtered by the army. So many people killed, always, over and over, in every land, across the world, butchering each other, neighbors and brothers. There we are all the same. This country, it is bloody too even though it be young. But they do forget, those who live here. They try to wipe it clean with skyscrapers and concrete. I think you are right Alek, about the ghosts. They are here. Many. I do feel it.

(Lights dim.)

Scene 4
The Bleachers. Early Morning.

> (**SAMUEL** and **ALEK** sit on the top bleacher watching. **JANE** is asleep in her deck chair. **MRS. STITKOVIC** is asleep on one of the bleachers. **DOMENIC** enters and moves over to **MRS. STITKOVIC** and nudges her awake.)

DOMENIC. Mrs. Stitkovic?

MRS. STITKOVIC. What? – I – where…?

DOMENIC. I'm sorry. I'm – I'm looking for Celia. We had – I wasn't happy how we left things yesterday and I wanted to see her again before I ship out. Can you wake her for me?

MRS. STITKOVIC. Yes, yes, of course.

> (Suddenly we hear blowing whistles, and clanging metal from off stage. **CHAZ, PRISCILLA, DIANA,** and **THALIA** come marching on tooting whistles and banging on pots and pans. **ZAHARA** is with them but not as vocal. They are holding placards: "Foreigner Go Home" "Bye Bye Bosnian" and "Proud To Be an American" The noise wakes **JANE**. She is very disoriented.)

PRISCILLA. We're here to join you Jane!

DIANA. *(chanting)* VI-O-LENCE!! VI-O-LENCE!!

THALIA. *(to **MRS. STITKOVIC**)* Go home, go home, go home!

DOMENIC. Whoa, whoa, girls…!

JANE. What is going on?

MRS. STITKOVIC. Lovelies, my lovelies, what is going on here?

CHAZ. Stay away from me!

PRISCILLA. We're starting a petition, and we already started calling parents, letting them know.

JANE. What are you talking about?

PRISCILLA. She doesn't belong here!

JANE. What?

PRISCILLA. She's Russian.

DIANA. Bosnian.

CHAZ. Shut up!

PRISCILLA. She's probably a spy!

JANE. *(laughing)* What?

PRISCILLA. I heard on the news or something that they're like poisoning people. Like in the food. The Russians.

MRS. STITKOVIC. I'm Bosnian.

THALIA. See? See? And like a terrorist.

JANE. What?!

PRISCILLA. She's Muslim.

JANE. So?

CHAZ. So?!

JANE. So her religion has nothing to do with what I'm protesting. She has nothing to do with what I'm – ...

PRISCILLA. Well, she's going.

CHAZ. You started it Jane, fighting for what you believe in.

JANE. No, no, this has nothing to do with what I be –

CHAZ. Now, we're just helping you finish it.

JANE. This is crazy! This has nothing to do with what I'm protes –

CHAZ. Oh, so you're defending her now?!

JANE. Yes actually.

MRS. STITKOVIC. Jane, don't –

DIANA. You shut up!

JANE. Diana!

DOMENIC. Hey, hey, hey –

MRS. STITKOVIC. Lovelies, lovelies...

THALIA. Stop calling us that!

(SYDNEY and CELIA come onto the field.)

SYDNEY. What is going on here?

CELIA. Dom, what are you doing here?

PRISCILLA. Oh great. More of the smart girls show up. Why don't you go stand over there with Jane and Mrs. S? We know whose side you're on.

SYDNEY. What are you talking about?

JANE. Okay, everybody let's just –

CHAZ. And you can just leave with her Jane since it's clear whose side you're on.

SYDNEY. What is going –

CHAZ. *(to* **MRS. STITKOVIC***)* I want you out of here. Muslim? Russian? Bosnian? Whatever.

DIANA. You don't belong here.

PRISCILLA. Yeah.

THALIA. And we don't want you here anymore.

DIANA. Yeah.

CHAZ. Pretending you're one of us. You'll never be one of us. So get out!

(She makes a lunge for **MRS. STITKOVIC***, getting her in a stronghold.* **DOMENIC** *tries to hold her back.)*

DOMENIC. Hey, hey hey…!

*(***DIANA** *starts hitting him.)*

DIANA. VIOLENCE!!!!!!!!!

(Suddenly the action freezes except for **SAMUEL** *talking to* **JANE** *and* **ALEK** *talking to* **MRS. STITKOVIC***. The women can speak but cannot move.)*

ALEK. *(to his mother)* You still want to stay in this country? Look how they turn on you.

MRS. STITKOVIC. Oh. Oh! *(laughing)* Thank you Alek. Just keep them like this and then I can do the escaping.

(She tries to move but can't.)

Alek? Alek? Help me to move.

ALEK. *(folding his arms)* Sorry. If this is your home now, you need to learn to live in it.

SAMUEL. *(to JANE)* See? This is your doing. You rile things up, and something's gonna happen that ain't right. Get outta here!

(He grabs her and pulls her out of the crowd.)

MRS. STITKOVIC. Stop that! Don't touch her! Alek, make me to move so I can help!

ALEK. Sorry.

MRS. STITKOVIC. *(to SAMUEL)* You must stop this! There are no boys allowed on the campus without permission.

SAMUEL. Hey, I'm not a boy!

(JANE gets away from SAMUEL. He chases after her.)

JANE. He's a ghost!

MRS. STITKOVIC. Oh! Alek, do you know of him?

JANE. *(to SAMUEL)* What are you doing? This is crazy.

MRS. STITKOVIC. Alek, at least do say something to stop him. Please!

ALEK. *(to SAMUEL)* Hello there my friend. Maybe it is better to not do the chasing and the pushing.

SAMUEL. I don't need advice from you…friend. Go haunt some other place.

ALEK. Oh, I am not haunting.

SAMUEL. Sure looks like haunting to me.

ALEK. It is just the visit.

SAMUEL. Then go visit someone else and leave my business to myself.

ALEK. My mother. She is worried about the girl.

SAMUEL. Oh, that girl can take care of herself.

MRS. STITKOVIC. Oh, that is the truth.

JANE. Thank you.

MRS. STITKOVIC. I knew from the first day of class.

ALEK. It is good to be strong.

SAMUEL. Wait. Wait! Enough with the chitchat! I got work to do.

MRS. STITKOVIC. I enjoy the chitchat. And Jane, you must have learned much from him. *(to* **SAMUEL***)* What is your name?

JANE. Samuel.

MRS. STITKOVIC. You should do the paper on him.

ALEK. Do not mention of having seen me please.

MRS. STITKOVIC. Oh Jane! This is my son Alek.

JANE. Hello, I –

SAMUEL. Stop it! Now! *(to* **JANE***)* Go! Go North. Run. Run away from here, but there ain't no place to hide from it, from me, from the history that hangs over this country. Now go!!

(He pushes her.)

MRS. STITKOVIC. Stop that!

JANE. Things can change. People can say, "This was wrong – is wrong. We were wrong." People can learn from mistakes, can't they?

SAMUEL. I see what I see. My family is here. Death is here. You can dress it up and play all the games you want on it and chitchat with all the niceties, but that's what I see. I'm done.

(The action suddenly starts up again.)

DIANA. VIOLENCE!!!!!!!!!

*(***DIANA** *lunges for* **MRS. STITKOVIC** *knocking* **THALIA** *into the tent. As* **DOMENIC** *tries to grab at* **DIANA**, **ZAHARA** *gets a hold of his gun.)*

ZAHARA. STOP!!!

(She turns the gun on the whole group.)

DOMENIC. Okay… Okay… Lets just –

ZAHARA. *(to* **CHAZ***)* Let her go.

(Nobody moves.)

Chaz!

*(***CHAZ** *lets* **MRS. STITKOVIC** *go.)*

MRS. STITKOVIC. Zahara…little lovely, what are you –

ZAHARA. This has to stop. This has to –

DOMENIC. It will – Let's just –

ZAHARA. I'm Muslim too. You wanna kill me? Like I'm sure they did to her family in Sarajevo, like they are doing to members of my family right now in Darfur.

CELIA. Darfur? What?

ZAHARA. Yeah. Big surprise huh?

CHAZ. What are you –?

ZAHARA. We, all of us – friends right? We really don't know anything about each other, so this is why we're here, right now.

SYDNEY. Ethnic cleansing.

ZAHARA. Muslims kill Muslims in Darfur just like in Iraq, but it's not about religion there. It's Arab against African. They don't care who you pray to. In Iraq how do they tell? In Rwanda, how did they tell? Here, right now, it's easy. *(She points the gun around.)* Should I kill her because she's white? Or him because he's in the military?

DOMENIC. Ok…ok…let's just, just calm down.

CELIA. Don't do this.

MRS. STITKOVIC. Shhh… Shhh…

JANE. Come on now… Zahara…? Come on. We can find a way to solve this.

ZAHARA. Yeah? How?

> *(The moment holds in tableau for a moment. Then **ZAHARA** turns to the audience. The rest of the cast stays frozen.)*

I didn't pull the trigger. It was Celia's brother who finally talked me down and got the gun from me. And no, I'm not in jail or anything like that. Being a diplomat's daughter has a lot of advantages. I went to college in Switzerland. I learned French and how to ski.

> *(**SYDNEY** speaks to the audience.)*

SYDNEY. I went into the Peace Corps. I thought I'd do it for a year and then go to college. But one year turned to two and then to three. I've seen things I never thought I'd see. Some things I never want to see again.

(DOMENIC turns and talks to the audience.)

DOMENIC. I didn't die over there if that's what you were expecting. I came home. I even went to school. For awhile. I didn't do drugs. I didn't start stealing. I don't like going outside. I watch TV I mostly watch cable so sometimes I forget what day it is. If you watch network TV you can tell what day it is by what's on but not with cable, and I really prefer cable. So the days get blurry. And my hand. It cramps up sometimes. From holding the remote.

(THALIA, PRISCILLA, DIANA, and CHAZ turn and speak to the audience.)

PRISCILLA. I went to school in California.

CHAZ. New York.

THALIA. I moved to Miami.

DIANA. I went traveling overseas.

PRISCILLA. Pepperdine.

CHAZ. NYU.

THALIA. I'm a receptionist at *Ocean Drive Magazine*. A lot of people want to work there, but I actually do.

PRISCILLA. The ocean is right there. I mean it's like in Malibu. I go to school in Malibu. How lucky am I?

CHAZ. There are so many people there. You know in that city. The City. That's what everyone calls it up there. And it sort of is. *The* City. At first I was really intimidated, but then I kinda liked it. Because there are so many people, there's always someone who's smarter or dumber or fatter or skinnier or shorter or taller, or thinks different than you, and you can hear like ten different languages walking down one block. Nobody's the same there. I like that.

DIANA. Nepal was my favorite place. I went trekking. When you walk for a long time, day after day, not talking, just walking, you realize the things you think. I didn't know before. I never realized what I thought about stuff. Now I do.

  *(**MRS. STITKOVIC** turns and talks to the audience.)*

MRS. STITKOVIC. I went home.

  *(**ALEK** starts humming the folk song and walking down the bleachers.)*

I started teaching again. And I taught the things I know. And I taught the things I learned while I was here.

  *(**ALEK** starts to walk offstage.)*

And I wait too, hoping, that maybe he will come back for another visit. But. Not so far. I lay flowers down in the spot we thought it was to be that maybe he had been buried. It is a green place. Peaceful. Who would to know that such ugliness could have been there? And we do not know really, where the grave is. There is no way to know. But I lay the flowers down there anyways, just in case.

  *(**ALEK** is gone.)*

  *(We hear the graduation march. Everyone leaves the stage except **SAMUEL** who sits on the top bleacher and **CELIA** and **JANE** who put on graduation gowns. They sit in the middle of the bleachers. The graduation ceremony has ended.)*

Scene 5
The Bleachers. Early Afternoon.

CELIA. Can you believe it?

JANE. Graduates.

> *(They high-five. Pause.)*

It was a good speech. You gave a good speech.

CELIA. Thanks.

> *(pause as they look out)*

It's really a beautiful spot.

JANE. I guess.

CELIA. I think so.

JANE. The first day I walked on this campus when we were freshman I thought it was the most beautiful place I'd ever seen.

CELIA. Yeah.

JANE. I see it differently now.

> *(SAMUEL stands up with some wild flowers in his hand. He walks down the bleachers.)*

CELIA. You think we'll come back for reunions and stuff?

> *(JANE looks at SAMUEL.)*

JANE. No. Let's not. I don't think I'll really need to come back.

CELIA. Same.

JANE. Let's just leave it for those who do then.

CELIA. Deal.

> *(SAMUEL places the flowers at the bottom of the bleachers on the ground.)*

Well, I should get going.

JANE. Yeah. Me too.

> *(CELIA and JANE stand and start walking off.)*

We didn't get along too well while we were here, did we?

CELIA. Nope.
JANE. I don't know why.
CELIA. Me either.

> *(They exit as* **SAMUEL** *walks back up the bleachers and sits at the top. Lights fade, lingering on the flowers for moment.)*
>
> *(blackout)*

End of Play

Aftershock

AFTERSHOCK was commissioned and produced in 2009 by Signature Theatre in Arlington, Virginia (Eric Schaeffer, Artistic Director, Maggie Boland, Managing Director) for their Signature in the Schools program (Marcia Gardner, Education Director). It was directed by Marcia Gardner, with scenic design by Walt Spangler, costume design by Guy Lee Bailey, lighting design by Mark Lanks, and sound design by Matt Rowe. The cast was as follows:

Q	Yasmine Boiragee
RUTHIE	Irene Casey
AYANA	Jamé Jackson
TIMOTHY/FATHER TIMOTHY	Michael Grew
MAKEMBA	Lintle Motsoasele
NEGIE	Brenda Nascimento
RUTH	Jocelyn Magsumbol
SARAH	Emily Johnson
PATRICK	John "Waffles" Morgan

CHARACTERS

Q – Female (could be male) 17. A slam poet.

RUTHIE – Female. 17. Inquisitive. Smart. Sensitive. Angry.

AYANA – Female. 19. African American. Passionate.

RUTH – Female 16. Jewish girl during the Holocaust. Haunted.

MAKEMBA – Female 16. From the Democratic Republic of the Congo. Smart. Protective.

NEGIE – Female 14. From the Democratic Republic of the Congo. Playful. Resourceful

SARAH – Female 14. A hidden child of the Holocaust in Belgium. Effervescent.

PATRICK – Male. 18. Smart. Goes where the wind takes him.

TIMOTHY – Male. 20. Works for the Red Cross. Compassionate.

FATHER TIMOTHY – Male. 30. Played by the same actor who plays Timothy. Caring.

SETTING

An American suburb. 2009.

Belgium. 1945.

New Orleans. 2005.

The Democratic Republic of the Congo. 2008.

Prologue

*(**Q** addresses the audience.)*

Q. After.
Shock.
Meaning a rumbling, a shaking, a quaking,
as in earth quaking,
a crack, crack, crackle, McCrackle of the earth,
deep, deep down below,
plates grinding
faults shifting,
saying, "No! Uh uh. Don't think so.
No more this.
No more that.
No more holding on to 'this is this' and 'that is that'
'cause maybe its time for this?
to be that. And that?
to be this.
Be-cause it's time.
time for change.
This re – re – releasing of the en – en – energy below
be-lowing up up, up,
to displace
the ground."
Displacement? A definition please.
"To move.
To force
from what is correct or usual."
I will add to that list – To move or to force from what is
comfort – able.

Comfort? I shall define
"Relief from pain or anxiety."
Hm. Yeah right. Sorry.
There is no comfort here.
Now I may be, according to Mister Webster, able as in
"physically
or mentally
e-quipped
to do something."
Fine that's me. I am all
of that.
But read on my friends
in the Dic-Tion-Ary
"Physically or mentally equipped to do something"
But the next part of the
de – Finitive de-Fi-ni- tion
in the Dic-tion-Ary
is the kicker, the rub, the downer, the party-crasher
the "Damn, what do I do with that?"
"Physically or mentally equipped to do something"
– especially because of circumstances or timing."
Well the circumstances suck.
My timing is poor.
I was not there for the quake, the initial rupture,
the main event,
the pain.
I could not shield from the quake.
I could not shelter in the storm.
I am here only for the After
Shock
They are smaller rumblings, yes.
But the initial quake did damage the foundation

>*(Lights up on **RUTHIE**, sitting on her bed staring at her laptop screen.)*

It did alter the core,
did leave a numbness to the fact
that the foundation has weakened,
is vulnerable and shaky and prone to
total De-struction of the Struc-ture
during what comes after
from the After-shocks.

> (**RUTHIE** *starts typing.*)

RUTHIE. *(typing)* "Whether it be the Holocaust, Hurricane Katrina, or current catastrophes such as the decades long war in the Democratic Republic of the Congo, survivors guilt is a real and devastating reality for those left behind…"

> *(She stops typing.)*

No, no, no, no… *(deleting)* Bad, bad, bad!

> *(She throws herself back on her bed. Lights shift back to* **Q**.*)*

Q. There is displacement in this place.

> *(Lights up on* **AYANA**, *arguing with a Red Cross worker [***TIMOTHY***] in New Orleans.)*

AYANA. I want some answers!

TIMOTHY. Ayana, that's your name right. Ayana?

AYANA. Yeah it is. Now answers!

TIMOTHY. I'm trying to give you as much infor –

AYANA. Try harder, okay? 'cause I don't see any effort here! I just see babies crying and people dying and no place to go to the bathroom! You gotta get us outta here, you hear me? You can't lock us all up here together like we're a bunch of animals or something! Saying you're with the Red Cross as if it means something! As if you're talking for God! Well, I don't see God here! That's the one thing I don't see! He went up and ran outta here as soon as those levees broke. God has gone and left New Orleans, and this is what we're left with?! You?! You, coming down here trying to give some comfort in his name. Shame on you! His name ain't written on this. This don't have nothing to do with him. 'cause the God I know? Woulda sent someone who knew what they were doing!

(Lights shift back to Q.)

Q. So
I am not able.
I cannot offer comfort.
So I – meaning me, myself, and I –
am not comfortable
in this chair,
this low, low, lying chair,
doing as the Jews do
when death comes knocking

*(Lights rise on **RUTH**, a Jewish teenager in 1945 Belgium. She wears a dress with a yellow Star of David on it. Q continues speaking as **RUTH** takes a knife and cuts the star from her dress.)*

From the cemetery, after burial, they return
To the home of the deceased.
They do sit
in the place where in life the dead did dwell.
For they say:
"Where a person lived there does his spirit continue to roam."
For seven days they sit.
They do mourn.
They do grieve.
They allow themselves to feel the pain.
They hang sheets
over mirrors.
No place for vanity here.

*(Lights rise on **MAKEMBA**, a teenager from the Congo. She has a regal quality to her. She is*

talking to her sister **NEGIE** *who is wrapped in a white sheet on a hospital bed.* **TIMOTHY**, *the same Red Cross worker we saw in New Orleans, tries to reach* **NEGIE**.*)*

TIMOTHY. Negie...?

(No response.)

MAKEMBA. Negie, answer him.

(No response.)

You don't have to be scared.

(No response.)

He wants to help you.

TIMOTHY. I want to help you.

(No response.)

MAKEMBA. Negie, please...?

TIMOTHY. Is there anything we can do to make you feel more comfortable?

(Lights shift back to **Q**.*)*

Q. There is no time for comfort here.
Only time to sit
and listen
and wait
This is what I will do.
For in my dis-comfort
I will be at the ready
to protect
to shelter
to comfort
as well as I can
for when the next shift,
the next tremor,
the next shock
o-ccurs...

Belgium: A Small Country Kitchen 1945

> (**RUTH** *enters. There is breakfast set for three people. She stops and stares at the food, surprised, anxious, hungry. She looks around making sure there is no one there. She grabs some bread and devours it while stuffing more bread into her pockets.* **FATHER TIMOTHY**, *a young priest, enters and sees her. He stops for a moment not wanting to startle or embarrass her.*)

FATHER TIMOTHY. *(in French)* Il y en a plus que assez. *[There's more than enough.]*

> (**RUTH** *immediately sits and shoves her hands in her pockets trying to hide what she's stolen, and she sits, her mouth closed tightly shut so he won't notice the food in her mouth.*)

(in French) C'est pas grave. Tu ne parles pas français je suppose? *[It's alright. You don't speak French I suppose?]*

> (*He now speaks German, which we hear as English because* **RUTH** *understands German, which means we can understand it.*)

I'll speak German then. You understand German, correct?

> (*She shakes her head slowly "yes."*)

I'm sorry I don't know any Polish, which I know is your native tongue, so German will have to do. It was good of your parents to teach you more than one language. Here in Belgium there is a whole section of the country that speaks only German, near the border. We speak mostly French here. And of course there is the Dutch speaking part of the country. So many here only speak the language from where they live. Strange for such a small country. I've made sure your sister speaks all three – Dutch, French, and German. I'll do the same for you if you'd like?

> (*No response.*)

And of course you'll both be able to speak German to one another. She came here so young and none of us speak Polish so... She lost a good deal of that skill it seems. It amazes me how without practice one can lose something that is such of part of who you are. Unfortunate I know. We'd all get along much better if we could all speak each other's language, don't you think? Maybe if there were just one common language, then it'd be harder to misinterpret one another, and then it'd be harder to disagree, and then maybe there'd be no war. Wishful thinking perhaps...

(No response.)

Would you like a bit of milk?

(RUTH doesn't move.)

It's for you. Please. There's more than enough.

(She reaches for the milk and begins to drink, gulping it down.)

The war is over.

(She stops drinking.)

That time is over. You're safe now.

(SARAH enters. She sees RUTH and stops, stares at her, and smiles.)

SARAH. Oh.

FATHER TIMOTHY. Ruth, this is –

(SARAH holds out her hand, waiting for RUTH to shake it.)

SARAH. Hello.

FATHER TIMOTHY. This is your sister Sarah. Sarah, this is Ruth.

SARAH. Hello.

(SARAH hugs RUTH who doesn't return the hug.)

FATHER TIMOTHY. Shall we pray?

(FATHER TIMOTHY sits at the head of the table. He clasps his hands and bows his head. SARAH does the same. RUTH does not move.)

FATHER TIMOTHY & SARAH. Bless us, O Lord, and these, thy gifts, which we are about to receive from thy bounty, through Christ, our Lord. Amen.

(FATHER TIMOTHY passes a basket of bread to SARAH. She takes a piece and hands the basket out to RUTH. RUTH just looks at both of them.)

SARAH. What's the matter with you?

FATHER TIMOTHY. Sarah.

(Lights rise again on RUTHIE's bedroom. She is having a restless sleep.)

RUTHIE. No...

SARAH. I haven't seen you in six years, we barely know each other, so alright if you want to be rude to me, but Father Timothy welcomes you into his home as a guest and this is how you act towards him?

(FATHER TIMOTHY stands and moves around the table toward SARAH.)

FATHER TIMOTHY. Sarah.

(RUTHIE tosses and turns.)

RUTHIE. No...

(FATHER TIMOTHY turns toward RUTHIE. His priest robes come off and he is underdressed in jeans and a black t-shirt. He is now TIMOTHY, RUTHIE's brother. He tries to wake her.)

TIMOTHY. Ruthie...

SARAH. The Old Testament certainly says something about being kind to a host, doesn't it, Father Timothy?

TIMOTHY. Ruthie...

SARAH. And you're my sister. You could at least speak to me after all this time and after all that's happened.

TIMOTHY. Sis.

SARAH. Fine. Sit there then. We'll eat this fine meal all by ourselves won't we Father?

> (*Suddenly* **RUTH** *says the Hebrew prayer that is said before eating bread, a little too loudly, with venom.*)

RUTH. Barukh ata Adonai Eloheinu melekh ha-olam, ha-motzi lehem min ha-aretz!

> (*She grabs a piece of bread and starts eating it.* **SARAH** *stares at her as* **TIMOTHY** *throws a pillow at* **RUTHIE**.)

TIMOTHY. Hey slacker!

> (**RUTHIE** *wakes up startled.*)

RUTHIE. Ah!

> (*Lights go out on* **RUTH** *and* **SARAH**.)

Ruthie's Bedroom

TIMOTHY. Wakey, wakey.

*(Disoriented, **RUTHIE** just stares at **TIMOTHY**, taking him in.)*

RUTHIE. Je-sus.

TIMOTHY. Nope. Just your big brother.

RUTHIE. What are you doing here?

TIMOTHY. You tell me.

RUTHIE. *(a little foggy)* I had a dream…with Grandma Sarah and Great Aunt Ruth – and – and you were a priest. They were fighting. Grandma – she was just…mean – and – and Auntie Ruth was being kind of a bitch.

TIMOTHY. Well you were named after her so that seems appropriate.

*(**RUTHIE**'s mood changes and she becomes combative.)*

RUTHIE. When did it become okay for you to start barging into my room? It's my room. I don't want you in here. Now get out.

*(**TIMOTHY** tries to tickle her playfully.)*

TIMOTHY. You just miss me 'cause I've been away so long.

RUTHIE. Yeah right. I haven't slept at all the last six days you've been home. Are guys just like incapable of not slamming a bathroom door and not stomping up and down the stairs and not clanging dishes in the morning? What is that? I can't get any freaking sleep since you've been back.

TIMOTHY. Mom and Dad don't seem to notice or mind.

RUTHIE. Yeah. Well. They're getting old just like you. They must be going deaf.

TIMOTHY. Everybody's waiting for you downstairs. Mom and Dad are getting pissed.

RUTHIE. They can start without me.

TIMOTHY. You have friends down there.

RUTHIE. They're here for you, not me.

TIMOTHY. No, they're here to see you. Come on.

RUTHIE. No. Get out. It's all for you anyway. Everyone will survive without me.

(She goes back to her laptop.)

TIMOTHY. Paper due?

RUTHIE. Yes, now go.

TIMOTHY. What's it about?

RUTHIE. What do you care?

TIMOTHY. I wouldn't be hanging around if I didn't care.

RUTHIE. Go. Please?

TIMOTHY. I'll be leaving soon enough so before we have to deal with everyone downstairs, I wanted to give you a little going away gift.

RUTHIE. Please, you're with the Red Cross, you're always going away, and you never gave me a gift before this, so save it.

TIMOTHY. Well, this time is a little different, isn't it? So, please – ...

(He takes out his wallet and starts to pull out an old, weathered photograph.)

This was something that Grandma –

RUTHIE. Don't.

TIMOTHY. I've had it for a long time but I think it really belongs to you. I've just been sort of safekeeping it, but this is the perfect time to give it to –

RUTHIE. What are you getting all brotherly on me for? *(pointing for him to leave)* Door, please.

TIMOTHY. I'm not going until you come downstairs. You don't go. I don't go.

RUTHIE. Fine.

(She doesn't move.)

TIMOTHY. Fine.

(He sits. She types. And deletes. Types. And deletes. He stands and wanders around the room. He picks up a framed photograph of the two of them.)

Hey remember this?

(She doesn't look up from her computer.)

You and me at the airport when I was going overseas for the first time. *(goading her)* I think you're crying in this one.

RUTHIE. Yeah right.

TIMOTHY. *(playfully putting the picture in her face)* Yep. Those are red eyes I see. And those are tears on your cheeks. Awww…

*(**RUTHIE** grabs the picture from him.)*

RUTHIE. Look! Stop it, okay? That was what, seven years ago? I don't remember it okay?

TIMOTHY. You don't remember how sad you used to get when I would go away?

(She turns on him and unleashes her fury/pain/confusion on him.)

RUTHIE. *(pointing at the photo)* Those are not tears. It was raining and I was mad 'cause it was July, and like, why did it have to rain in July? I wanted to go to the beach, and Mom and Dad said we had to wait to go to the beach because we had to take you to the airport, and I was like, "Can't he go to the airport by himself 'cause I want to go to the beach," but they said you were going far away and that there were little kids like me there who needed you, and it was really sunny all morning but we couldn't go to the beach because of you. They kept saying, "We'll go after we take your brother to the airport," and then as soon as we got there to drop you off, it started to rain, and I knew we wouldn't get to the beach at all that day, and I was really pissed at you just like I am now, so those were not tears, those were raindrops. I wasn't sad. I wasn't sad then when you went away, and I'm not sad now. In fact you going away would make me really, really, happy. So please just do it. Get out of my room. I don't want you here.

TIMOTHY. That's a lot of stuff to remember about a something you have no memory of.

RUTHIE. You. Are annoying.

TIMOTHY. I. Am your big brother. That's what we do.

RUTHIE. You know what? I'm telling Mom and Dad. I'm going down there with all those people standing around and, I'm gonna tell Mom and Dad what you're doing.

TIMOTHY. Fine. Go tell 'em. Go tell 'em I'm up here bothering you. Let's see what they say.

(RUTHIE starts to leave, then stops.)

RUTHIE. Oh...! Smart. Uh, uh. Sorry brother. Nice little trick but –

(She sits back on her bed.)

I said I wasn't going down there. I'm not.

TIMOTHY. Ruthie. You have to.

RUTHIE. No I don't. I can't.

TIMOTHY. Why?

RUTHIE. I have to finish this paper.

TIMOTHY. Looks to me like you haven't even started it.

RUTHIE. Exactly. So if you would just get out of here and leave me alone, then maybe I could actually get some work done.

TIMOTHY. And then you'd go downstairs?

RUTHIE. I – ...What?

TIMOTHY. What if I wrote it for you? Sort of.

RUTHIE. Excuse me?

TIMOTHY. Look, if I don't get you out of here and get you down there, Mom and Dad will – well, I don't want to see what that'll be like so... It's a little selfish on my part too. We get it written, you go downstairs.

RUTHIE. What if we don't?

TIMOTHY. Then I guess you can just stay up here forever.

RUTHIE. And you'll leave me alone?

TIMOTHY. And I'll leave you alone.

*(***RUTHIE** *holds her hand out.)*

RUTHIE. Deal.

*(***TIMOTHY** *shakes her hand.)*

TIMOTHY. Done. So. What does this paper have to be about?

RUTHIE. Well it has to be about a world event. Political. The aftermath of a political event. Like about the survivors. About how people survive tragedy. How they move on or don't move on or something like that.

TIMOTHY. Interesting. You should write about Grandma and Aunt Ruth.

Belgium. 1945. Ruth's Bedroom

(**RUTH** *lies on her bed staring at the wall.* **SARAH** *enters with a bowl of soup. Hearing* **SARAH***'s voice,* **RUTH** *sits straight up on the side of her bed.*)

SARAH. Father Timothy thought you might still be hungry after eating so little at breakfast.

(**SARAH** *puts the bowl of soup down.*)

RUTH. No thank you.

SARAH. You can't live on only bread.

(**SARAH** *waits for a response. She doesn't get one. She starts to leave and then turns back.*)

(with an edge) Do you like your room?

RUTH. Yes, thank you.

SARAH. In the morning you never have to worry about being late for school because the sun shoots through the windows and hits your face just right to wake you up. There's more sun in this room than any room in the entire convent. All the sisters envy it. And the view? I don't think there's a more beautiful view in all of Belgium. We thought it'd be best for you. We thought you might like it. This used to be my room. That used to be my view and my sun, but now it's yours. No need to thank me for it.

RUTH. I did say thank you, and you can have it back. I don't want it.

SARAH. We were trying to be nice. I'm *trying* to be nice. To be understanding. *I'm* trying to be a good sister.

RUTH. I don't need you feeling sorry for me.

SARAH. I – …! Never mind.

(*She goes to leave again.*)

RUTH. I *can* live on only bread! I can live on rotting, molding bread that has bugs burrowing through it. I can live on half eaten bread, that still has bloody saliva on it from the dead person lying in the bunk next to me whose fist I pried it from. Take the soup away, and bring me a bowl of dirty water. They gave us that and called it soup. Don't feed me at all. I'll go outside and survive on snow like I did when they stopped feeding us all together. Take back your room. I've slept on splintered wood with just a paper-thin blanket crawling with lice to shield me from the cold. Take that away from me, and I'll still survive. I don't need it. And I don't need you.

(SARAH picks up the bowl of soup and starts to leave.)

If this is my room, then take the crucifix off the wall please.

SARAH. This is a convent. There are crucifixes in all the rooms.

RUTH. I'm a Jew. I don't want it here.

SARAH. And I'm a Catholic now.

RUTH. I see that.

(Pause. SARAH contemplates taking the crucifix down. Then:)

SARAH. If you don't want it there, take it down yourself.

Ruthie's Bedroom

RUTHIE. No way. Not that story. Too depressing.

TIMOTHY. No it's not.

RUTHIE. Um, the Holocaust is freaking depressing. Next.

TIMOTHY. Why don't you write about me?

(beat)

RUTHIE. What?

TIMOTHY. I've seen a lot of survival. Nice to know you pay attention to your brother's life.

RUTHIE. Oh. That.

TIMOTHY. Yeah. That.

RUTHIE. So…

TIMOTHY. Okay. I got a good one. Down in New Orleans after Katrina, there was a girl.

*(**RUTHIE** starts typing.)*

RUTHIE. New Orleans.

*(Lights rise on **AYANA**.)*

TIMOTHY. She was kind of like you actually?

RUTHIE. Really?

TIMOTHY. She dealt with things that happened to her by getting angry too.

RUTHIE. I'm not angry!

TIMOTHY. Okay.

RUTHIE. Who said I was angry about anything?

TIMOTHY. Sometimes people have the right to be angry.

RUTHIE. Well I'm not. So. There.

TIMOTHY. Fine, fine, you're not angry.

RUTHIE. I'm not.

TIMOTHY. Well Ayana was.

New Orleans – The Superdome

*(Lights up on **AYANA** as we saw her earlier. She is again taking it out on **TIMOTHY**.)*

AYANA. Shame on you! His name ain't written on this. This don't have nothing to do with him. 'cause the God I know? Woulda sent someone who knew what they were doing!

TIMOTHY. The Red Cross isn't a religious organization.

AYANA. Oh really now?

TIMOTHY. Yes, and you're right about me not knowing what I'm doing.

AYANA. 'scuse me?

TIMOTHY. I – I've never seen anything like this. And I've seen a lot. All over the world. But here. In America… I never thought I'd see it here.

AYANA. Well, you need to get out more.

TIMOTHY. Pardon?

AYANA. "Pardon." Educated white boy coming down here to take care of those of us who were lucky enough to live.

TIMOTHY. No. That's not what – …I can understand how you would feel that way but –

AYANA. No you can't. You can't understand how I feel, or how I live, or what I've been through.

TIMOTHY. *(to **RUTHIE**)* So she told me.

AYANA. There was a party. My brother was having a hurricane party. We'd been through storms before. My parents had been through a lot of 'em. And there were warnings, yeah, but nobody was coming to take us out. They just told us we had to go but… How were we gonna pay for six of us to travel and then get hotel rooms? So we *had* to stay really. What else were we gonna do? That night my older sister wasn't answering her phone, so my parents went over to her house to get her and my niece to bring 'em back to our place so they'd be safe. They never came back. I've been looking, but I don't know where they're at... And back at the house – the water just came. So fast. And my brother and all his friends had been partying and drinking and they were laughing at first, playing in it, but the water just kept rising, and I was screaming for all of them to get upstairs. I was at the top of the stairs trying to pull my brother with me but then there was just this surge of water and it pulled him from me, and – I just had to keep going. I tried. I did. I kept trying to grab his hand, but the water kept getting higher and higher, so I – I had to save myself. I climbed out the top window on to the roof. It was so dark. Couldn't see a thing. But I could hear – the screaming – all of them screaming from underneath the water. But I couldn't do nothing. I couldn't help any of 'em. So I just sat there, covering my ears and shutting my eyes. Not moving. Just waiting. Not sleeping. Just waiting. Waiting for the light. God's light, 'cause I knew I was gonna die. And the light did come, just not the kind I was expecting.

TIMOTHY. *(to* **RUTHIE***)* When the sun rose the next morning she saw that she wasn't alone.

The Lower 9th Ward of New Orleans: A Rooftop

*(Lights up on **AYANA** on a rooftop. **PATRICK** is passed out on the edge of the roof.)*

AYANA. Wake up. You! Wake up!

PATRICK. *(waking up disoriented)* What, what, what?

AYANA. Who are you?

PATRICK. What…? I – …What?

AYANA. What's your name?

PATRICK. Patrick – I'm – …I'm Patrick.

AYANA. What are you doing here?

PATRICK. Where am I?

AYANA. You're on my roof. Now, how'd you get here?

PATRICK. What? What's going on?

(He finally looks at his surroundings.)

Aw Jeez! What – What the hell is going on?

AYANA. Start talking. How did you get here?

PATRICK. I came out here to smoke. Darryl said we couldn't smoke in the house.

AYANA. You were at the party?

PATRICK. And the rain. I mean it was really coming down. Felt good though. I must've passed out.

AYANA. Passed out?! What else were you smoking?

PATRICK. Oh…this and that.

AYANA. How do you know my brother?

PATRICK. I go to Tulane and he works in one of the dining halls and well, we started talking, yesterday. All my friends went home 'cause of the storm. Their parents made them come home, but I just got here, and well, I didn't want to fly all the way back to California, and my parents were pissed. They said they were flying down here to come get me whether I liked it or not. I wonder where they are. Jeez, I wonder where they are.

AYANA. They probably couldn't get a flight in.

PATRICK. Oh my father got in. If he had to rent a private plane, he got in.

AYANA. Oh. Oh, I see. Well, you don't got a thing to worry about then. He's probably hanging out in a suite at the Ritz Carlton eating caviar watching the weather channel. Why don't you have daddy rent a helicopter and come over here and save us?

PATRICK. Save us? ...Where's Darryl? Where – where's everybody else? Where are they –?

AYANA. It's just you and me, okay? So don't say one more thing about it or ask about anybody in there, you hear me? Just keep quiet about it.

(It takes a few moments, but finally PATRICK realizes what she's saying.)

PATRICK. Oh my God... Oh my God...

AYANA. Quiet.

(Lights shift back to RUTHIE's bedroom.)

TIMOTHY. *(to RUTHIE)* They didn't talk much after that. They just waited, hour after hour in the hot sun on that boiling roof.

(Lights shift back to the rooftop. We hear the sound of a helicopter overhead. PATRICK is lying down on the roof. He doesn't look well. AYANA is waving her arms in the air.)

AYANA. Hey...! Hey...! We're right here! *(to PATRICK)* Hey, why don't you help me? Maybe if they saw the white boy calling for help, they'd get us outta here quicker.

PATRICK. I – ...I can't.

AYANA. What do you mean you can't? I haven't eaten either but I'm up here screaming my brains out.

PATRICK. I'm just really wiped out.

AYANA. Well so am I. Now get up.

PATRICK. No really I can't.

AYANA. Come on.

(She bends down to get him up. He rolls over and throws up.)

Aw Jeez… Hey… Hey…

(She rubs his back.)

You okay?

PATRICK. Ummm… Yeah, yeah. It's cool.

AYANA. You're dehydrated. All this sun and no water. That's why we gotta get someone to rescue us.

PATRICK. Just give me a minute.

(She sits.)

This sucks.

AYANA. Sucks? *(laugh)* Yeah. Yeah, it does.

*(**PATRICK** looks out.)*

PATRICK. I knew New Orleans before I got here. I studied it. Books, photos, maps. It's where I wanted to be. As far away from Orange County as I could get. No more big lawns and swimming pools.

AYANA. Can I ask you? Seriously. What could ever be wrong with big lawns and swimming pools?

PATRICK. Everything always being the same, knowing nothing's ever gonna be different for you.

AYANA. We got lots of that here too. Only the view ain't as pretty.

(We hear a very distant helicopter.)

Hey, hey, you hear that? Come on, get up.

PATRICK. I can't stand up. You're gonna have to do it yourself.

AYANA. Aw, no, no, no, get up here and help me.

PATRICK. No really I can't.

AYANA. What?

(He doesn't say anything.)

What is going on?

PATRICK. I'm a diabetic.

AYANA. What?

PATRICK. I need to take insulin and well…

AYANA. You're kidding me right?

PATRICK. Believe me, I wish I was. It's back at my dorm. I didn't take it with me.

AYANA. What?!

PATRICK. I was just going to a party. I only thought I'd be gone for a few hours. I was just going to a party.

AYANA. Jeez, what kind of a screw up are you?

PATRICK. Hey, look, is this really the time to –?

(The helicopter is getting closer.)

AYANA. I don't have time for this, okay?

PATRICK. I know –

AYANA. I don't have time to be looking out for you and your stupidity while I got all this mess to think about.

PATRICK. Hey, while you're tearing me a new one, maybe I'll go into shock or a coma and then you won't have to worry about my stupidity anymore.

AYANA. Oh great. Now look what you got me thinking about.

PATRICK. Look, we really don't have time for this –

AYANA. No, no we don't! You could die you know. You could freakin' die, and I don't have the time or the energy to deal with that!

(The helicopter sounds is very loud. AYANA stands and tries to wave it down.)

Hey…! HEY!!!!!!

(The helicopter keeps going, not stopping.)

Damnit! You're gonna get me killed! I am gonna die, and it's gonna be all your fault!

(She sits. There is a long silence between them.)

PATRICK. Do what you have to do.

AYANA. What?

PATRICK. You might not get rescued for days still.

AYANA. *We* might not.

PATRICK. Listen to me. A dead body can – get in the way. It can be unpleasant. The smell.

AYANA. What are you talking about?

PATRICK. The sun's real hot. And it's gonna stay hot.

AYANA. Stop it.

PATRICK. You don't need anything lying around reminding you about what could happen to you.

> (**AYANA** *can just look at him.*)

My name is Patrick. Patrick Sullivan.

AYANA. What are you doing?

PATRICK. Patrick Sullivan. Remember that.

AYANA. Stop it.

PATRICK. My parents' names are Jerry and Patricia. Jerry and Patricia Sullivan from Costa Mesa, California. Let them know. So they don't have to wonder. So they don't have to wait.

AYANA. No. We can still fix this. We can.

> (**AYANA** *starts waving her arms toward the sky even though there is no helicopter.*)

Hey! …

PATRICK. There's no one there.

AYANA. Another one will come by. I can hear it. Can't you hear it?

PATRICK. No. No one will come in time.

AYANA. HEY!!!! …

PATRICK. Nobody's coming.

AYANA. Somebody?! …ANYBODY?!!!

> (*The lights go down on* **AYANA** *and* **PATRICK.** *Lights up on* **RUTHIE**'*s bedroom.*)

TIMOTHY. No one did come. Not that day. Not that night. And not for two days and two nights after that. Three mornings later, when a rescue team finally did arrive, it was too late for Patrick. I met Ayana in the Superdome. That's where I was, trying to help survivors and she told me her whole story.

New Orleans – The Superdome

(We see **AYANA** *telling her story to* **TIMOTHY**.*)*

AYANA. I'm sorry, but I won't feel sad that some rich, white kid's dead. At least it wasn't one of us this time. At least it wasn't someone who was poor or black or who had been shot down by life a thousand times before. He was there because he thought it'd be cool to go to some party in the crummy part of town. He could've got out. He could've left before the storm hit. It's not my fault he didn't.

TIMOTHY. No it's not.

AYANA. I held his hand while he died.

TIMOTHY. That was kind of you.

AYANA. And I cried, sitting there holding his hand.

TIMOTHY. That's natural.

AYANA. And I hate it. I hate that I cried sitting there, holding his hand, while he died in the sun on the roof of my house in the Lower 9th Ward of New Orleans. Him talking all romantic about that city I was born in, that I never got to leave. I used to pray for it. I used to pray the whole stinking place would get wiped away. And there it was right in front of me. The whole city flooded. And I sat there and I cried for him. And then I stopped 'cause I realized that I hadn't cried one tear for my family yet. That ain't right, that he should get my tears first. And then he started to stink, so I pushed him off the roof just like he told me to, and I watched him float away. I survived. The only one from my whole family. I gotta live with that. I *don't* have to live thinking they're looking down seeing me crying for a total stranger instead of them.

Ruthie's Bedroom

(**RUTHIE** *has stopped typing.*)

RUTHIE. Wow.

TIMOTHY. Yeah.

RUTHIE. I can't write that.

TIMOTHY. Yes you can.

RUTHIE. No I can't.

TIMOTHY. People have to survive any way they can, even if it's ugly, even if it means being angry for a long time, like you being angry at me.

RUTHIE. It's not the same thing.

TIMOTHY. Hey, I kept my part of the bargain. Now we go downstairs.

RUTHIE. No.

TIMOTHY. That was the deal.

RUTHIE. The deal was I had to finish the paper. I don't want to write that story, so the paper isn't finished. So. I don't go downstairs.

TIMOTHY. Hm. Sneaky.

RUTHIE. No. Just smart.

TIMOTHY. Okay then… Negie and her sister Makemba.

RUTHIE. Wait. What?

TIMOTHY. Another story. I'm going to win this little sister.

RUTHIE. I don't want to hear another story.

TIMOTHY. Are you forfeiting then?

RUTHIE. No. Your first one didn't cut it, so I win.

TIMOTHY. Nuh, uh, uh. That's not how it works. But if you're scared I'll come up with something that'll make you lose…

RUTHIE. I'm not scared.

TIMOTHY. Then type. Negie and her sister Makemba would play hide and seek in the jungle that lay on the edge of their village in the Congo.

A Forest in the Democratic Republic of The Congo

> (**MAKEMBA** *and* **NEGIE** *play hide and seek.*)
>
> (**MAKEMBA** *whistles.*)

NEGIE. Come out! Makema, come out, I give up!

MAKEMBA. Shhh… Not so loud. They'll find us. Do you want to go back there right now?

NEGIE. No. I'm tired of chores.

MAKEMBA. Yes, yes, chores I'm tired of chores too. Let's keep playing. I'm right here. You can find me and then it'll be my turn to find you.

NEGIE. But I can't. You're voice seems to be here and there and everywhere all at once.

MAKEMBA. You're just being foolish. Open your ears and you'll find me.

> (*She whistles again.*)

NEGIE. Oh, I know now!

> (*She runs in the opposite direction of where* **MAKEMBA** *is.*)

MAKEMBA. No! No, not that way. You're heading straight back to the village. This way. Follow my voice.

NEGIE. You're playing games with me. I can't tell where it's coming from. Just come out and show yourself.

MAKEMBA. No, that ruins all the fun. Come on, you can do it. Follow my voice.

> (*She whistles again and* **NEGIE** *follows in the right direction.*)

That's right. Keep going. Keep going. You'll find me yet.

> (*Lights shift from the sisters to* **RUTHIE**'s *room.*)

TIMOTHY. Makemba convinced her sister to sneak away day after day.

*(**MAKEMBA** whistles and the lights shift to the sisters playing hide and seek again.)*

MAKEMBA. Come on now you're getting lazy. Hurry, hurry, follow my voice.

NEGIE. We're going to get in trouble. Mother and father are going to guess we've been sneaking away.

MAKEMBA. You're just angry because you can never find me.

NEGIE. Wait. Did you hear that sound?

MAKEMBA. Yes.

NEGIE. It sounds like footsteps.

MAKEMBA. It's probably father. Hide, Negie, hide. If he finds us, we'll get a beating.

NEGIE. No, I want to go back. He'll be less mad if we just tell him now why the chores aren't done. And besides, you never let me find you anyway. You always get to hide, and I always have to look. I want to go back. *(calling off)* Father!

MAKEMBA. You can hide now. Negie, you can hide. Do it now, and I'll have to find you. Would you like that? Would like me to have to find you?

NEGIE. Maybe…

MAKEMBA. Do it now. Hide now. And don't move. Don't move from your hiding spot.

NEGIE. You always move. That's why I can never find you.

MAKEMBA. I know. But I've been cheating. You want to win for real, don't you? You want to win without cheating right? You'll be the winner then. If you can stay in one place and not be found then you'll be the all time winner.

NEGIE. I'd like that.

MAKEMBA. Well that can't happen if father finds us, so hide, Negie. Hide now. The footsteps are getting louder.

NEGIE. It sounds like more than one persons footsteps.

MAKEMBA. Mother is probably with him and she'll be twice as mad as he'll be when she finds out we've been playing instead of doing our chores.

NEGIE. You're right.

MAKEMBA. So hide, Negie. Now! Before they find you.

> (**NEGIE** *crouches and hides. They each are silent for a few long moments.*)

NEGIE. Do you think they're –?

MAKEMBA. Shhh.

> (*a few more long silent moments*)

They're gone.

NEGIE. Good. Now you have to find me.

MAKEMBA. Already did.

> (*She taps* **NEGIE** *and quickly runs to hide without* **NEGIE** *seeing her.*)

NEGIE. How did you do that?

> (**MAKEMBA** *laughs.*)

NEGIE. It's not fair. You're quicker.

MAKEMBA. That's true. So come and find me my sister.

> (*She switches her hiding place.*)

NEGIE. Hey, you're moving again. I can tell. Your voice is moving.

MAKEMBA. That's right.

NEGIE. So you can still cheat, but I couldn't?

MAKEMBA. That's right.

NEGIE. Alright then. I'll still find you. Even with you cheating, I'll still find you, and I'll win.

MAKEMBA. *(laughing)* Follow my voice. Follow my voice.

> (**MAKEMBA** *runs off and* **NEGIE** *follows her. Lights shift back to* **RUTHIE**'s *room.*)

TIMOTHY. They played the game day after day after day.

(Lights shift to the girls still playing their game. **NEGIE** *is physically exhausted.)*

NEGIE. I'm tired of this Makemba. It's the same game day after day, and I can never find you. This is getting as dull as our chores.

MAKEMBA. Just a little while longer, and then we can stop. Then we don't have to play the game anymore.

NEGIE. Where are we? You've taken us too far into the forest. I don't recognize any of this. Where are we?

MAKEMBA. Just a little while longer.

NEGIE. Then we can go home?

MAKEMBA. Just a little while longer.

(Lights shift back to **RUTHIE***'s bedroom.)*

TIMOTHY. I remember when I first met Negie. She could barely walk she was so exhausted. She had been walking for weeks. And she wouldn't speak to me.

(Lights rise to reveal **NEGIE** *wrapped in a sheet like at the beginning of the show.* **MAKEMBA** *stands next to her.* **TIMOTHY** *tries to reach* **NEGIE**.*)*

Negie…?

(No response.)

MAKEMBA. Negie, answer him.

(No response.)

You don't have to be scared.

(No response.)

He wants to help you.

TIMOTHY. I want to help you.

(No response.)

MAKEMBA. Negie, please…?

TIMOTHY. Is there anything we can do to make you feel more comfortable?

MAKEMBA. Tell him what happened to you Negie.

TIMOTHY. Would you like to tell me what happened?

(NEGIE doesn't move.)

How did you get here?

(NEGIE doesn't respond.)

It was very brave of you to walk all that way alone.

(NEGIE doesn't respond.)

Any time you need to talk, I'll listen.

(He starts to move off.)

NEGIE. I wasn't alone.

TIMOTHY. What?

NEGIE. Where is my sister? Where is Makemba?

TIMOTHY. Your sister?

(NEGIE goes silent again.)

Negie, you walked in here alone two days ago.

MAKEMBA. Tell him Negie.

TIMOTHY. Please tell me what happened to you.

MAKEMBA. You remember. You must tell him.

NEGIE. I can't.

MAKEMBA. You must.

NEGIE. No.

TIMOTHY. Who are you talking to Negie?

MAKEMBA. Tell him about that day. You remember. The day we played hide and seek for the very first time.

TIMOTHY. Negie?

MAKEMBA. Remember? We were playing hide and seek.

NEGIE. *(to* **TIMOTHY***)* We were playing hide and seek.

*(**NEGIE** finally speaks to **TIMOTHY** as **MAKEMBA** coaches her through the story, helping her remember.)*

MAKEMBA. You always asked me, begged me –

NEGIE. I always asked Makemba. Everyday I would beg, "Can't we sneak away just for an hour?"

MAKEMBA. You were tired of chores

NEGIE. I was so tired of chores. "Our brother can do the chores all my himself. He is the oldest. Let's go play."

MAKEMBA. I always said, "No."

NEGIE. She always said, "No."

MAKEMBA. And then after day upon day of badgering finally I said yes.

NEGIE. She said yes.

MAKEMBA. You picked the game.

NEGIE. "Hide and seek," I said. "I want to play hide and seek."

MAKEMBA. I hid first.

NEGIE. We were running and hiding.

MAKEMBA. You couldn't find me.

NEGIE. I couldn't find her.

MAKEMBA. Then there was a sound.

NEGIE. There was a very loud sound.

MAKEMBA. The birds scattered.

NEGIE. The birds screamed and flew away.

MAKEMBA. Leaves fell down on us.

NEGIE. They flew away so fast.

MAKEMBA. The sound seemed to come from the village

NEGIE. It came from the village.

MAKEMBA. Sound after sound after sound.

NEGIE. They were gunshots. So many, gunshots.

MAKEMBA. Then we heard screams.

NEGIE. It was my mother.

MAKEMBA. We ran.

NEGIE. We ran back toward the village.

MAKEMBA. The militias had come.

NEGIE. There were soldiers.

MAKEMBA. They burned the village.

NEGIE. Our home was on fire.

MAKEMBA. They were shooting all the men.

NEGIE. Our brother was dead on the ground.

MAKEMBA. And our mother...

NEGIE. Soldiers surrounded our mother. Then they were on top of her, one after another. They had a gun to our father's head and made him watch. Makemba grabbed my face and said.

(MAKEMBA grabs NEGIE's face as if it were that day.)

MAKEMBA. "No matter what happens, you don't move. Do not move. You stay here. You hide. Do you hear me? You hide. No matter what happens."

(She runs off.)

NEGIE. And Makemba ran out to try and save my mother from what was happening to her. My father screamed, "Makemba, no!" Somehow he freed himself for a moment and ran toward her, and then there was a machete...and blood...and my father was – he – ... My mother was still on the ground, splattered with my father's blood, her head turned toward me. Silent. She was alive but not alive as soldier after soldier... Only when they grabbed Makemba and laid her down between my mother and our father's headless body, and the soldiers started on my sister, only then did my mother scream. It rattled the trees and the ground and the sky. I hid just as my sister made me promise. I held my hands over my ears to try and block out my sister's and my mother's screams. It went on for hours. Then I heard two more gunshots. Their screams stopped. I did not move. I just hid. I did not move. I don't know how many days or nights I stayed there. Then one day I heard...

(MAKEMBA "whistles".)

MAKEMBA. Come Negie. Let's play hide and seek. Come find me Negie. Follow my voice. Follow my voice...

(Lights shift to RUTHIE's bedroom.)

Ruthie's Bedroom

(**RUTHIE** *stops typing.*)

RUTHIE. Wait. I don't understand.

TIMOTHY. What?

RUTHIE. So Makemba died, right?

TIMOTHY. Yes.

RUTHIE. Negie was hiding and saw – heard what happened to Makemba. She was there when her sister died.

TIMOTHY. Was murdered.

RUTHIE. And then suddenly they're playing hide and go seek day after day in the forest?

TIMOTHY. People need to survive any way they can.

RUTHIE. You mean Makemba was just in Negie's imagination?

TIMOTHY. Can you think of a more resourceful way of getting through the forest night after night, soldiers everywhere who might kill you? Why not play a game with your dead sister? A game that'll keep you moving and hidden all at the same time.

RUTHIE. That's crazy.

TIMOTHY. No it's smart.

RUTHIE. Whatever.

TIMOTHY. And maybe she didn't imagine her sister. Maybe she was really there.

RUTHIE. What, like a ghost?

TIMOTHY. Why not? Maybe Makemba really did come back to help her little sister out.

RUTHIE. That'd make her even crazier.

TIMOTHY. Are you crazy then?

RUTHIE. What?

TIMOTHY. Which kind of crazy are you?

RUTHIE. What are you doing?

TIMOTHY. Am I a ghost, or am I just in your imagination?

RUTHIE. Don't.

TIMOTHY. You're not staying up here because you have a paper to write.

RUTHIE. Don't you do this.

TIMOTHY. You don't want to go downstairs because everyone – Mom, Dad, the whole family, your friends – everyone is down there sitting shiva.

RUTHIE. What?

TIMOTHY. Oh come on. I know you're not the best Jew in the world but sitting shiva? The seven days of mourning after a person dies.

RUTHIE. Stop.

TIMOTHY. I'm dead.

RUTHIE. I said stop it.

TIMOTHY. I died in a car crash last week driving here from the airport. I was coming home for a visit.

RUTHIE. You *are* here visiting.

TIMOTHY. No. No one else sees me but you. That's because they've all accepted the fact that I'm dead.

RUTHIE. Go away. Go into the light or…wherever it is you're supposed to go.

TIMOTHY. *(laugh)* That only works in the movies.

RUTHIE. I won't let you do this. I won't.

> *(She runs out of her room and heads downstairs. She runs into* **Q** *in the kitchen.* **TIMOTHY** *follows her.)*

Q. Whoa.

RUTHIE. Hey Q.

Q. Hello my friend. You look like you just saw a ghost.

RUTHIE. What?

Q. I'm really sorry about your brother.

RUTHIE. Yeah, yeah, thanks. Thanks for coming.

Q. We've been worried about you. I've been coming by every day but your parents said you wouldn't come out of your room.

RUTHIE. Yeah, I'm sorry about that.

Q. No. It's all good. You gotta do what you gotta do.

RUTHIE. Where are my parents?

Q. In the living room.

RUTHIE. Can we stay in here? I can't deal with seeing them right now.

Q. Sure.

> *(They go and sit at the kitchen table that was used for the scene between **RUTH** and **SARAH** that we saw earlier. They sit silently for a bit.)*

RUTHIE. Did you really come by every day?

Q. Sure.

RUTHIE. Why?

Q. You're my friend.

> *(beat)*

I got some writing done.

> *(She hands her notebook to **RUTHIE**. **RUTHIE** opens it and reads from it.)*

RUTHIE. "Aftershock."

Q. It's kind of inspired by you.

RUTHIE. "After.

Shock.

Meaning a rumbling, a shaking, a quaking

As in earth quaking

A crack, crack, crackle, McCrackle of the earth."

Q. I'll let you read the rest later. Still working on it.

> *(Pause. **Q** puts the other notebooks she's been holding on the table. They are weathered and worn.)*

Your Mom showed these to me. They were your brother's, from all of his trips. He had some amazing stories.

TIMOTHY. Wrote 'em all down.

RUTHIE. Shh!

Q. What?

RUTHIE. Nothing.

Q. You should check 'em out.

> (**TIMOTHY** *takes a small notebook out of his pocket, takes the weathered photo out of this wallet and slips it into the notebook.*)

They're really amazing.

> (**TIMOTHY** *slips the small notebook into the pile of notebooks on the table.* **RUTHIE** *tries to grab it before* **Q** *sees it, but* **Q** *grabs it.*)

Hey, I didn't see this one.

> (*She opens up the notebook. The picture falls out.*)

Who's in this picture?

> (**RUTHIE** *takes the picture.*)

RUTHIE. Those are my great grandparents in the back, and that's my grandmother Sarah, the little girl on the right, and that's my great Aunt Ruth on the left. I was named after her.

Q. Wow. A namesake.

RUTHIE. Yeah.

Q. So are you like her?

RUTHIE. I never met her. In the Jewish religion you're not supposed to be named after someone who's still alive. It's bad luck.

Q. Hm. I can see that.

RUTHIE. Yeah, I don't know much about her or my grandmother really – just that they survived the war. She'd talk to my brother about it. She'd show us this picture all the time. She said, "This is your family. This is all that's left to remember that time and that place. You should know the stories." But I never... I just... I'd get bored. She said, "One day this picture will be yours. Our family heirloom. The only thing left. One day I'll give it to you." She gave it to my brother instead.

Q. But now he's given it to you.

TIMOTHY. I'm giving it to you.

> (**Q** *flips to the first page of the notebook.*)

Q. Hey, he dedicated this story to you. "For my sister Ruthie, daughter of Miriam, granddaughter of Sarah, named after Ruth sister of Sarah." The story's called –

TIMOTHY. "The Kitchen Table."

> (**Q** *holds the story out so they can both read it.* **RUTHIE** *just stares at the pages.*)

Q. *(reading)* "The kitchen table. The table in my parents kitchen is very old."

TIMOTHY. Almost seventy years old.

Q. "It's got a lot of miles on it."

TIMOTHY. It came all the way from Belgium.

Q. "It was built by a priest."

TIMOTHY. "By Father Timothy, the man I was named after."

Q. "Mom and Dad say –"

> (**RUTHIE** *interrupts and takes over reading the story.*)

RUTHIE. "Mom and Dad say that Grandma Sarah and Auntie Ruth always talked of him, of how he shielded them after the quake, how he sheltered them from the storm, how he offered comfort in a time when that word seemed to be erased from the dictionary. "A comfort giver," my mom and dad thought. "That's what we want our son to be."

TIMOTHY. "And so that's how an upper middle class Jewish boy from America was named after a Roman Catholic priest from war torn Europe. Grandma used to love to tell about the time Auntie Ruth first saw the table."

> (**RUTH** *appears in the kitchen. It is late at night. She is hungry looking for food.*)

RUTHIE. "About how she hadn't seen so much food in so long. Of how she first saw her sister Sarah, and about how my grandmother –"

TIMOTHY. "Sarah."

   (SARAH appears watching RUTH.)

RUTHIE. "– first saw her sister Ruth."

TIMOTHY & Q. Your namesake.

RUTHIE. "They had not seen each other since they were young children. They were strangers, and at that first meeting they fought and then sat silently over breakfast. They fought later that day over food, and bedrooms, and God, which was the only way they could avoid saying what they really wanted to say. Then later that night…"

   (RUTH finds a piece of bread and then notices SARAH. She hides the bread behind her back.)

SARAH. Hungry?

RUTH. No, I told you.

SARAH. You lie.

RUTH. I'm going to bed.

   (RUTH goes to leave.)

SARAH. What's in your hand then?

RUTH. Nothing.

SARAH. You lie.

   (RUTH puts the piece of bread on the table.)

RUTH. I don't need it.

   (She goes to exit again.)

SARAH. "Whither thou goest I will go."

   (RUTH stops.)

RUTH. What?

SARAH. "Whither thou goest I will go. Your people shall be my people."

RUTH. What are you –?

SARAH. From the *Book of Ruth*. When Ruth's mother in law loses everything, both of her sons, Ruth goes with her so she won't be left alone in the world. Ruth says to her,

"Whither thou goest I will go. Your people shall be my people."

RUTH. Yes, I know the story.

SARAH. I used to make Father Timothy read it to me all the time because I knew that you were named after her. And I'd say to him, "My sister is Ruth. She will not desert me. She will come find me. She will come and be with me."

RUTH. I couldn't.

SARAH. You all left me.

RUTH. Mama and Papa did what was best for you. Would you rather have come with us to the ghetto where we were crammed with dozens of others in two tiny rooms, begging for food, praying every day that we wouldn't be put on one of those trains.

SARAH. You were together.

RUTH. Until the camps. You should be on your knees praying to your new God every night thanking him for giving you such loving parents.

SARAH. I don't remember them! How can I be thankful for something I can't remember? You shouldn't have let them send me away, and when they did, you should have followed. "Whither thou goest I will go. Your people shall be my people." I had no people here. I tried to hold on to something – to some memory – of Mama with her head covered lighting candles I think and of Papa with that funny little cap on his head. But they faded. I can't remember their faces. I had to become someone else just to feel like anybody at all.

RUTH. You don't want to remember our parents as I do. I only see them as I last saw them. You don't want to remember that…

(Pause. They both sit at the table.)

SARAH. This morning when you got mad at me and you said those words? What were those words?

RUTH. It was Hebrew.

SARAH. Oh. Yes, of course.

RUTH. It was the blessing we say before eating bread.

SARAH. I don't remember anything.

>*(**TIMOTHY** holds up the weathered photograph. **SARAH** takes it from him.)*

See this? Father Timothy gave it to me as a little girl, the first night I came here.

RUTH. Mama and Papa couldn't risk you carrying anything. It couldn't look like you were going into hiding.

SARAH. I had nothing. But Father Timothy gave this photograph to me, and he told me *(pointing at the photograph)* this was you and this was me and there were Mama and Papa. Those aren't any of us of course. But he gave it to me and told me it was my family, so I decided to believe.

RUTH. That was kind of him.

SARAH. He's a kind man. I would look at the photo every night, these strangers hugging each other and laughing and I made up my own memories of us. All of us happy, smiling, and laughing.

>*(beat)*

Thank you for finally coming.

RUTH. I couldn't come any sooner. I couldn't…

SARAH. Maybe… Maybe we can forgive one another.

RUTH. Yes.

SARAH. Will you teach me?

RUTH. What?

SARAH. Teach me one of your prayers.

>*(**RUTH** picks up the bread and coaches **SARAH** through the prayer.)*

RUTH. Barukh ata Adonai…

SARAH. Barukh…

RUTH. Barukh ata Adonai…

SARAH. Barukh ata Adonai…

RUTH. Eloheinu melekh ha-olam…
SARAH. Eloheinu melekh ha-olam…
RUTH. Ha-motzi lehem min ha-aretz.
SARAH. Ha-motzi lehem min ha-aretz.

> (**RUTH** *picks up the bread, tears it in half, gives half to her sister, and they eat.* **RUTHIE** *closes the notebook.*)

Q. Wow. You have an amazing family.
RUTHIE. Yeah. Yeah I do.

> (**TIMOTHY** *kisses* **RUTHIE** *on the head and leaves.*)

Q. You should really find your parents.
RUTHIE. Yeah. Can I just have a minute in here alone?
Q. Sure.

> (**Q** *leaves* **RUTHIE** *alone at the table staring at the photograph.* **Q** *addresses the audience.*)

Their stories – they ripple.
They vibrate.
They shock,
Saying, "Listen and learn.
Remember my name
Remember my story.
Remember it all.
Not just war, and famine, and terror, and death.
Remember joy, and survival, living, and life.
And when someone says,
"Oh how sad," during the next war
or the next famine
or the next "How could such a thing *be*
in this world
in this place
in this time that I live?"
Say "No." No talking. No crying. No beating of the breast.
I will not standby

as a by-stander
I will do.
I will work.
I will lift and shove and pull
to stop the next "next."
I will block it out
Erase the word.
Scratch its De-Fi-Ni-Tion
From the Dic-Tion-Ary.
Don't say "next" to me
I won't listen
I wont hear.
Instead I'll hear their names.
Names.
They vibrate through the air,
like how aftershocks from a quake,
how they ripple through the earth.
I feel the ripples
I hear the names
Ruthie and Miriam

SARAH. And Sarah

RUTH. And Ruth

TIMOTHY. And Timothy

NEGIE. And Negie

MAKEMBA. And Makemba

PATRICK. And Patrick

AYANA. And Ayana

Q. I hear the names.

AYANA. Ayana

PATRICK. Patrick

MAKEMBA. Makemba

NEGIE. Negie

TIMOTHY. Timothy

SARAH. Sarah

RUTHIE. Ruthie
RUTH. Ruth
Q. And I?
   I am Q.
   Just one letter. Q.
   Q – for the question –
   Who are *you*?

End of Play

Shakespeare, Will

SHAKESPEARE, WILL was originally commissioned and produced in 2010 by Signature Theatre in Arlington, Virginia (Eric Schaeffer, Artistic Director, Maggie Boland, Managing Director) for their Signature in the Schools program (Marcia Gardner, Education Director). It was directed by Marcia Gardner and the assistant director was David Zobell, with scenic design by James Kronzer, costume design by Diana Khoury, lighting design by Mark Lanks and sound design by Matt Rowe. The cast was as follows:

NARRATOR	Anne Veal
WILLIAM SHAKESPEARE	John Morgan
POPPI	Irene Casey
KYRA	Houda Bekkali
ALIX	Jamé Jackson
OLIVIA	Loreal Watts
J.J.	Brenda Nascimento
TEESHA	Lintle Motsoasele
CHLOE	Jocelyn Magsumbol
CAT	Alexis Lodsun
ANNE HATHAWAY	Anne Veal

CHARACTERS
(in speaking order)

NARRATOR – A pre-recorded female voice for the documentary that starts the play. Can be done live.

WILLIAM SHAKESPEARE *(goes by* **WILL***)* – The world famous writer at the age of 18.

(All of the following students are female and of high school age.)

POPPI – A good student. Very involved in school activities.

KYRA – Wise beyond her years. A quiet strength that comes from necessity.

ALIX – Passionate. She is always ready for a debate. She is counting down the minutes to graduation so she can start living the life she knows she's meant to live.

CHLOE – Pretty and knows it. Not dumb at all and savvy enough to know that "pretty" can put you one step ahead of the pack in life.

CAT – Very smart. An independent thinker. Aware of what is going on around her even if her head is always stuck in a book. Only speaks when it is necessary. Dry sense of humor.

OLIVIA – Doesn't stand for bull from anyone. Can seem not interested and sometimes combative, but that's really just the armor she wears.

J.J. – Likes high school life. Popular. More going on inside of her than she lets out.

TEESHA – A definite side kick to J.J. They are practically a team. A follower who should be a leader.

ANNE HATHAWAY – Shakespeare's wife. 26 years old. Eight months pregnant. Very smart and very fiery which aren't the ideal traits for a woman to have in the 16th century if she wants to find contentment.

SETTING

The present. An all girls' high school in northern Virginia.

Prologue

*(In the darkness we hear sweeping, grand, overly emotional, pretentious music: the underscoring for a documentary. A few seconds into the music a voice mixes in with the music. The **NARRATOR** speaks with a Masterpiece Theatre, British accent. The following lines that she recites overlap each other slightly. The lines should be done in a sonorous tone – like they're terribly brilliant and undeniably important.)*

NARRATOR. *(voice over)*

"To be or not to be. *That* is the question."[1]

"Oh, Romeo, Romeo. Wherefore art thou Romeo?"[2]

"Beware the ides of March."[3]

"If we shadows have offended,
Think but this and all is mended..."[4]

"By the pricking of my thumbs,
Something wicked this way comes..."[5]

"Oh for a muse of fire...!"[6]

---

[1] *Hamlet* 3.1 56
[2] *Romeo and Juliet* 2.2 33
[3] *Julius Caesar* 1.2 18
[4] *Midsummer* 5.1 417
[5] *Macbeth* 4.1 44
[6] *Henry V* Prologue 1

Scene One

A High School Class Room

(Lights rise on a classroom. **GIRLS** *sit at their desks watching the documentary that we are hearing. They all have different responses to it.* **POPPI** *sits, enthralled and totally entertained.* **ALIX** *is sitting on the back of her chair, ferociously watching, but she is aghast and appalled by what she is seeing and hearing.* **CHLOE** *is too busy doing her nails to even listen to the movie let alone watch it.* **OLIVIA** *is asleep with her head on her desk.* **CAT** *is reading* The Bell Jar *by Sylvia Plath.* **KYRA** *watches the movie placidly.* **J.J.** *and* **TEESHA** *sit at adjacent desks and are texting each other from their iPhones.)*

NARRATOR. As you have seen in the past ninety minutes –

> (**ALIX** *looks down at her watch.*)

– it is virtually impossible to measure the worth of this great man and his monumental body of work. I know you all are thinking, as am I, "How is such a thing possible? How could such a man have lived? And how did he give birth to all that he created?" To answer that question, I come back to those immortal words that begin his great play *Henry the Fifth.*

(very grand) OH FOR A MUSE OF FIRE!

I like to imagine him as a young man –

> *(Lights slowly rise on* **WILLIAM SHAKESPEARE** *in silhouette.)*

– before success comes, perhaps before he has written a single play – alone at his desk, unable to write, wondering what possible spring the words will burst forth from, hoping against all hope that he will find a way – not knowing he will one day be the greatest dramatist the English speaking world will ever know.

But how was he to see all this back then? He was just a young man named William Shakespeare, staring at a blank page, crying out for inspiration in the dark.

WILL. *(with quill pen pointed to the heavens)* OH FOR A MUSE OF FIRE!

> *(A final flourish of towering, bombastic, John Williams-like music. The movie ends.* **POPPI** *starts applauding.* **J.J.** *and* **TEESHA** *turn the lighter app on their iPhones and hold them up in the air and make the muffled sound of a huge crowd cheering.* **OLIVIA** *remains asleep.* **KYRA** *claps politely then reaches into her bag to check for messages on her phone. She has none. She focuses back on the unseen teacher.* **POPPI** *raises her hand high and enthusiastically. The unseen teacher calls on her.)*

POPPI. Yes, thank you Mr. Fisher. I…*loved* it. I mean, what an inspiration. I just – and I found it really, really, moving, didn't you?

> *(***ALIX** *stares right at the unseen teacher and very slowly raises her hand as* **POPPI** *continues.)*

And at the end when they were asking about, how, you know, how he did it. How did he write all those plays? I was thinking the exact same thing at the exact same time that they said it. Like in my head it was like, "Oh my God, how did he do it?" and just as I was thinking it, they were saying it, and I was just like, "this is weird. This must mean something." And I got that burning feeling behind my eyes like maybe I'm gonna cry, 'cause that happens to me sometimes. A burning. Right behind my eyes. And if I squeeze them real tight or rub them, it goes away and I won't cry, but if I just stare straight ahead, not even blinking, just eyes wide open, staring straight ahead, sometimes it'll actually happen for real. Sometimes I'll cry. So I'm not lying about me being moved by it. I was. I really, really was.

> *(***KYRA** *raises her hand, and she is immediately called on.)*

KYRA. Yes, I found some of the historical aspects fascinating and informative, but I thought the presentation of the material was a little cold.

POPPI. Oh I didn't. I didn't at all Mr. Fisher. I think it was a really good choice.

> (**ALIX**'s *hand is now fully raised. The unseen teacher calls on her.*)

ALIX. Yes, thank you Mr. Fisher I do have something to say. I most definitely have some things I'd like to say about the movie.

> (*She reaches into her backpack and pulls out a huge book.*)

I have some things I'd like to say about the general subject of Mister William Shakespeare.

> (*She drops a huge volume of* The Complete Works *on her desk, making a loud thud. The sound wakes up* **OLIVIA** *suddenly.*)

OLIVIA. (*startled but precise and "at attention"*) William Shakespeare, born April twenty third, fifteen ninety-four, died April twenty third, sixteen-sixteen! That means he died on his birthday!

> (*Everyone looks at her.* **J.J.** *and* **KEESHA** *burst into laughter.* **OLIVIA** *stands up and stares them down.*)

(*threatening*) Hey!

> (*The laughter stops.* **OLIVIA** *sits down.*)

ALIX. I mean is this film supposed to inspire me to read *King Lear*? Is this supposed to get us all excited to learn about Shakespeare? This long winded, not particularly informative –

POPPI. I thought it was informative. (*to the teacher*) I feel very informed.

ALIX. Poppi, it was made in the 60s. Haven't some new ideas about his life come along? Hasn't there been more research, new discoveries, some *real* scholarship on the man –

J.J. Alix, we're not in college yet.

TEESHA. That is the truth.

J.J. We all know you can't wait to go.

TEESHA. Your bags are packed.

J.J. But some of us don't mind it here.

TEESHA. I certainly don't.

J.J. Some of us like high school.

TEESHA. I do.

J.J. And some of us actually think we're learning something of value.

TEESHA. Well, I don't know about that.

ALIX. May I continue?

J.J. Would it matter if I said –

ALIX. No.

TEESHA. It would not.

J.J. Well, I don't understand you getting all worked up. It's just a movie.

ALIX. It's obnoxious.

POPPI. It's beautiful.

CHLOE. *(not looking up from her nails)* It's boring.

OLIVIA. It's a bunch of pasty face British people talking funny.

J.J. Oh, I like those English boys' accents.

TEESHA. Yeah the accents.

J.J. Sexy.

TEESHA. Very.

ALIX. Okay! Let's forget about the movie then.

J.J. Thank God.

TEESHA. Amen.

*(**ALIX** opens up The Complete Works.)*

ALIX. Let's just take a look at this then shall we? If you just look at the table of contents, you begin to notice something very interesting.

J.J. Meaning?

TEESHA. Meaning?

ALIX. *Meaning.* All these plays are about men.

CHLOE. What?

POPPI. No.

ALIX. Yes.

OLIVIA. There's Juliet.

POPPI. Exactly. There's Juliet.

KYRA. She's a girl.

CHLOE. *(still doing her nails)* A pretty, pretty, girl.

ALIX. She's an and.

J.J. & TEESHA. What?

ALIX. She's an and. *Romeo AND Juliet. Antony AND Cleopatra. Troilus AND Cressida.* And that's it my friends. They're the only women in any of the titles. Three. That's it. Three! *And* they're all ands. It's all King this and King that. And on top of all that, they all kill themselves over some guy.

CHLOE. That's romantic.

ALIX. That's psychotic.

CAT. That's inaccurate.

  (beat)

ALIX. Excuse me?

CAT. *(barely looking up from her book)* Cressida doesn't kill herself for Troilus. In fact she doesn't even die.

ALIX. Oh. Well. Nobody knows that play anyway.

CAT. So there's Kate.

J.J. & TEESHA. Who?

CAT. Kate, in *The Taming of the Shrew.* Kate is the shrew in *The Taming of the Shrew.*

ALIX. That's the best that he can do? 'Cause I don't see the name Kate anywhere in that title. I only see Shrew. The shrew. That's it. She's just a shrew. Shrew: a woman of violent temper or speech. I looked it up.

J.J. Someone in the room just picked up a nickname.

TEESHA. MmHm.

ALIX. What I'm saying is –

POPPI. What she's saying Mr. Fisher is that she is fired up.

ALIX. Excuse me?

POPPI. She is moved to action now. She has a great idea about a group project we can all do together.

ALIX. Poppi what are you –

POPPI. Mr. Fisher can I talk to you for a second? *(to* **ALIX** *under her breath)* Listen, I need him to write me a good recommendation, so just keep quiet for a minute and let me handle this.

(She walks off to talk to the teacher.)

J.J. Group? Group project?

TEESHA. What's that all about?

OLIVIA. I don't like doing things in a group.

CHLOE. Are we going to have to build something? Cause my nails are not in a place where I can start building things right now.

J.J. Building? With like wood and nails and stuff?

TEESHA. Not cool.

CHLOE. I cannot get any splinters, so if that could happen, then just count me out.

OLIVIA. I really don't like doing things in a group.

ALIX. Guys! I don't know what she's talking about. I have nothing to do with it.

*(***POPPI*** comes back.)*

POPPI. Ok. So.

ALIX. What was that all about?

POPPI. Don't you dare! You get him all riled up, and you know when he's mad at one of us, he gets mad at all of us. Well I can't handle a bad grade in this class right now.

(**KYRA**'s *phone starts ringing. She goes to answer the call.*)

I don't think any of us can so –

KYRA. *(answering the phone)* Hello…? *(to the* **GIRLS***)* I gotta grab this.

(She starts to exit.)

POPPI. Everything cool?

KYRA. Um, still don't know yet.

POPPI. Find me as soon as you hear.

KYRA. Ok.

(She starts to exit.)

POPPI. And Kyra if I don't see you, meet us today at 5:00 in the theatre.

KYRA. Got it. I'll be there.

(She exits.)

OLIVIA. Whoa, whoa, whoa. The theater?

POPPI. Yeah, what's the problem?

J.J. Well, it's like a construction zone at the moment.

TEESHA. Scaffolding

J.J. Dust.

CHLOE. Dust? I can't handle dust. And what are we gonna do if something falls or something and one of us gets killed?

OLIVIA. Ok, I'm really not up for getting killed.

J.J. No one is allowed in there.

POPPI. So. Cat has a key. Cat, you have a key right?

ALIX. What? Poppi actually breaking the rules?

POPPI. Yeah. Yeah, okay?! You all don't know me at all. Just be there. In the theatre at 5:00.

> *(Everyone starts giving her excuses of why they can't be there or simply just telling her that they don't want to come, get hurt etc. They become quite the vocal crowd.)*

Hey!! We do this guys unless you all want to write twenty-five page papers on William Shakespeare – his life and times, which is what Fisher was going to throw at all of us because of you know who over there.

ALIX. Hey!

POPPI. QUIET! Just do it. Okay? Just do it. Jeez! And be on time.

> *(Everyone scatters except* **CAT** *who is on the last page of* The Bell Jar. *She finishes the book, sighs contentedly, closes the book, and then looks up to discover she is alone.)*

CAT. Hey, where'd everybody go?

> *(blackout)*

Scene Two

On the Stage of the School's Theater

(POPPI is standing on stage, tapping her foot, clearly annoyed. CAT wanders in reading Kerouac's On the Road.*)*

POPPI. Why is everyone in the world always late for everything?

(CAT doesn't even look up from her book.)

CAT. *(almost dead pan)* No one's late. It's you who's early. You're always early, so to you everyone else is always late.

(She sits and continues reading. KYRA enters talking on her cell phone.)

KYRA. Yes, yes, I'll keep my phone on, so just call or text if you hear anything... Love you too.

(She hangs up. POPPI goes over and squeezes her hand.)

POPPI. Still no news?

KYRA. Nope.

(ALIX comes in with OLIVIA just behind her. KYRA moves to put her things down.)

OLIVIA. How long is this gonna be 'cause I got things to do.

ALIX. Now can you let us know what this is all about?

(J.J. and TEESHA enter both frantically texting and don't' even look up from their iPhones as they address POPPI.)

J.J. Shut up.

TEESHA. We're not late.

J.J. You're just early.

TEESHA. Shut up.

J.J. We're not late.

ALIX. Can we start?

OLIVIA. I got things to do.

POPPI. Chloe isn't here yet –

CAT. She's late.

POPPI. Well I need everyone here so –

CAT. It's five.

POPPI. I know but –

CAT. On the dot.

POPPI. Okay will you –

CAT. You're the one obsessed with time.

POPPI. I know but –

CAT. Start!

POPPI. Hi there ladies! So. Instead of doing long, tedious, boring, papers, I came up with what I think is a really brilliant idea. I thought we could put on a show where we all do some scenes from Shakespeare.

(Silence.)

What do you think? It's great right?

ALIX. This is what I came here for?

J.J. Acting is cool. It's better than doing a paper if you ask me.

TEESHA. Ask *me* then.

J.J. Is it better than doing a paper Teesha.

TEESHA. MmHm.

OLIVIA. I'm not doing anything where I gotta stand up in front of people. If I wanted to be dramatic, I'd join Drama Club.

KYRA. I play the lute.

J.J. & TEESHA. What?

POPPI. Musical accompaniment! That's perfect. What a great idea. Good for you Kyra. Good. For. You.

CHLOE. Okay, fine, so we do a little acting, we have a little music, but aren't you forgetting one major problem?

POPPI. Yes! We're going to need a stage manager.

(**CAT** *raises her hand without even looking up from her book.*)

Good Cat, you're it, and I'll get Fisher to give you credit for doing that.

CHLOE. Aren't there like a lot of guys in his plays?

ALIX. Hello! Look at the titles people, look at the titles!

POPPI. Exactly. So… And this is the exciting part. We'll play the boys too.

J.J. & TEESHA. What?!

(**KYRA***'s phone rings. She grabs it.*)

KYRA. Gotta grab this. I'll be back.

(*She exits on her phone.*)

Yeah, hi Mama.

CHLOE. Well, I'll go along with it, but I have to be Juliet.

OLIVIA. Why do you get to play Juliet?

CHLOE. Well look around. Who else is pretty enough to play her?

OLIVIA. Someone is going to take you out one day.

CHLOE. And there's no way I'm playing a boy.

J.J. I don't wanna play a boy either.

TEESHA. No way.

J.J. Why can't we all be girls?

TEESHA. 'cause, after all, that's what we are.

J.J. And let's get some real boys in to play the boys.

TEESHA. Yeah!

POPPI. No see, this is the special thing about it. We go to an all girls' school, so we do Shakespeare with all women just like they did back in his time, except back then it was all guys.

J.J. & TEESHA. What?

POPPI. That's the way it was. So we can get some great brownie points for the cleverness of the idea right? I'm so smart.

ALIX. What are you talking about?

POPPI. Oh please, don't tell me that you don't know how Shakespeare's plays were done during his lifetime.

ALIX. Umm. I don't okay?

J.J. Wow.

TEESHA. Amazing.

J.J. There's something you don't know?

TEESHA. Who woulda thunk?

POPPI. All the actors back then were men.

ALL. *(except* **POPPI** *and* **CAT***)* What?!

POPPI. It's true.

OLIVIA. No way.

ALIX. Cat, help us out here? Give me some facts.

(**CAT** *looks up from her book.*)

CAT. They were guys.

J.J. & TEESHA. No

CAT. All of 'em. All the actors were ac – TORS. No tresses to be found.

CHLOE. Oh can you please speak English normally for once in your life?

CAT. Pick up a book and check it out for yourself. It's historical fact. They were guys. Every single one. Juliet, Cleopatra, all of 'em, played by guys.

ALIX. Well, that's just wrong. Can't you see how completely and totally wrong that is?! Like all the girls played by guys. That's like…not right.

CAT. Wow. When did you get all homophobic?

ALIX. Oh please! I am so not that, and you know it. I'm talking about simple fairness. Equal opportunity. Fifty/fifty. Cause if it's not gonna be like that, if we're not going to decide that that's the way the world should be, then why don't we just say, "Hey, let's have a white guy play Othello!"

CAT. Oh that's happened too. Over and over. Historically. In black face even.

ALIX. See?! That's as bad as burning crosses. That's why people take to the streets in the thousands saying, "No more! We won't take this anymore!" So why is this any different? It's still someone getting something when someone else doesn't 'cause of something they didn't have any say about.

J.J. & TEESHA. Huh?

ALIX. We're girls okay. We didn't get a choice in that, and we keep getting less because of it, right? And this is just one more thing. Just one more thing we women got shut out of in the long tedious, unfair, history of the... – See? See?! It's right in the word. HIS-tory. His. Story. Figures.

(She goes to write that down.)

CHLOE. Well herstory just sounds stupid, so that was never gonna work out.

POPPI. OKAY FINE! We'll just do all girl scenes then. Jeez!

(She goes into her backpack and pulls out stacks of paper that she hands out.)

I try to do something interesting and clever, I do all the work on it, the research, and the copying, in THREE hours mind you, and then half of it's going to get tossed away, 'cause god forbid we do something as horrible as speaking some of the greatest language ever written because it was written for boys!

(She tosses a huge stack of paper in a garbage can.)

ALIX. Okay now, you don't have to get all –

POPPI. And you! I thought you'd be the first to want to read some of these male scenes. If you want to go all feminist on us then I'd think you'd be clawing to read *Hamlet* or *Richard the Third* to show that idiot Shakespeare that we can do things just as good as the boys!

ALIX. Good point.

POPPI. Really?

ALIX. BUT! I'm protesting against the man himself. I don't like him okay? So I'm not reading any of his language, no matter who it's written for.

POPPI. Then you're gonna fail.

ALIX. No I won't. I'll be the director.

POPPI. The director? How can you be the director if you hate the man's work?

ALIX. A director needs to have some distance from the material. My detachment will be good for the project.

POPPI. Oh. Okay then. Director.

(She hands over some pages.)

Direct.

ALIX. Okay. Umm… So Teesha you read *(pronouncing wrong)* Hermya.

CAT. *(not looking up from book)* Hermia.

ALIX. And J.J. you read *(pronouncing wrong)* Heleena.

CAT. Helena.

J.J. So what are we supposed to do?

TEESHA. Yeah.

ALIX. Act.

POPPI. Oh *that's* a brilliant bit of direction.

TEESHA. *(looking at the pages)* Can we do something that's in English?

J.J. What does "Fie" mean?

TEESHA. What?

J.J. Look, I gotta say "fie."

OLIVIA. Like Fee Fie Foe Fum?

TEESHA. Well, I gotta say "canker blossom."

CHLOE. Eeeww. Now that's just nasty.

J.J. What language is this?

POPPI. It's English guys.

OLIVIA. Sounds British to me.

POPPI. Oh Herr Director, are you going to do something, maybe help out a bit, and let everyone know what's going on in the scene?

ALIX. Well...

> *(pause)*

CAT. Look, Hermia is in love with Lysander and Lysander is in love with her. Helena is in love with Demetrius but Demetrius is in love with Hermia, and he's been given Hermia's hand in marriage by her father, and if she doesn't marry him, Dad's allowed by law to kill her.

OLIVIA. Whoa.

CAT. So Hermia and Lysander run away into the woods so they can be together. Demetrius follows Hermia, and Helena follows Demetrius. Puck, who's like a sprite and Oberon, who's like king of the sprites give the guys love potions to make them fall in love with the right woman, but it all ends up going wrong and both the guys end up crazy in love with Helena, and nobody loves Hermia, and she's really ticked about it, now go!

> *(A little scared of her, the **GIRLS** immediately start reading the text really fast but with no meaning.)*

TEESHA AS HERMIA. O me! You juggler! You canker-blossom!
You thief of love! What, have you come by night
And stole'n my love's heart from him?'

J.J. AS HELENA. Fine, i'faith!
Have you no modesty, no maiden shame,
No touch of bashfulness? What, will you tear
Impatient answers from my gentle tongue?
Fie, fie, you counterfeit! You puppet, you!

> *(They stop and look up for some response. **ALIX** hands pages to **POPPI**.)*

ALIX. Here.

POPPI. What?

ALIX. Direct.

(**OLIVIA** *picks up her backpack and starts leaving.*)

POPPI. Where are you going?

OLIVIA. I'm going to start writing my twenty-five page paper.

POPPI. No. Hey, hey. We can do this. I know we can. We can't be brilliant right away. But with a little time and a little practice, I bet we can be great. And I have an idea.

ALIX. Is it as good as this first one?

POPPI. Now. We need to do something together as a cast, as a company, some sort of ritual to bond us together. I think we should read some Shakespearean text together on this our first rehearsal. We'll be like calling out to the spirit of Shakespeare himself, asking for his help and guidance. Sort of like a blessing.

ALIX. Oh brother.

POPPI. Now everybody come and let's stand in a circle.

(*No one moves.*)

(*suddenly very harsh*) Come on GUYS, DO IT! JUST DO IT! NOW, NOW, NOW!!!

(*Everybody but* **CAT** *jumps up and stands in a circle.*)

CHLOE. You know you can be scary sometimes?

POPPI. (*suddenly very sweet*) Cat, are you going to join us?

CAT. (*not looking up from her book*) I'm the stage manager. The stage manager doesn't have to do the circle stuff.

POPPI. Fine. Now everybody join hands.

[7]Double, double toil and trouble;

(*silence*)

Come on, just say it!

Double, double toil and trouble

EVERYONE. (*but* **CAT**) Double, double toil and trouble

POPPI. Fire burn, and cauldron bubble.

---

[7] *Macbeth* 4.1 35

EVERYONE. *(but* **CAT***)* Fire burn, and cauldron bubble

POPPI. Cool it with a baboon's blood
 Then the charm is –

CHLOE. Eeewww! That's just nasty.

ALIX. Oh brother...

OLIVIA. That ain't a blessing.

J.J. What kind of blessing is that?

TEESHA. That's just wrong.

POPPI. No, no, it's from one of his plays. There are these witches see?

J.J. Witches?

CHLOE. Eeewww!

TEESHA. That's wrong.

OLIVIA. What did you just have us do?

POPPI. Guys, it's just some text that is said by these characters –

ALIX. Witches.

POPPI. Yes, but they say it all together so I thought – Look, I can pick different text from another play if that'll make you feel better.

> *(***KYRA** *enters. She looks distracted, preoccupied, upset.)*

KYRA. What's going on?

ALIX. Poppi's casting spells

POPPI. It's not a spell. I'm using some of Shakespeare's text as a sort of blessing for the space, to bring us good luck.

KYRA. A blessing? Can I say it with you?

POPPI. Sure! Thanks. Hey are you okay? Looks like you've been crying.

KYRA. I'm fine. Can we just do the blessing?

OLIVIA. I wouldn't' do it Kyra. There's something creepy evil going on in those words she's saying.

POPPI. Guys, come on it's from one of his plays.

OLIVIA. Which one?

POPPI. The Scottish play

J.J. The whatta play?

ALIX. That's not in the table of contents. I would've remembered that.

POPPI. Well it's not really called the Scottish play

OLIVIA. Then why are you calling it that?

POPPI. Because you have to

J.J. & TEESHA. What?

POPPI. It's bad luck if you say the real name.

ALIX. What are you talking about?

POPPI. It's true. You can't say the name of the play in the theatre or bad things will happen.

ALIX. What play?!

CAT. *(not looking up)* Macbeth.

POPPI. *(huge gasp).* You didn't.

CAT. I did.

POPPI. Cat?!! You are like the *worst* stage manager who ever lived!

ALIX. What is going on?

POPPI. Look, this is *really* serious guys. It's bad luck to say that word in a theater.

TEESHA. What word?

POPPI. The word she just said.

CAT. Macbeth.

POPPI. CAT?!!!! Okay now, we gotta move fast. In order to reverse the bad luck, the person who said the word – CAT! – has to exit the theater, spin around three times, say a curse word, and then ask for permission to come back inside. It also helps to say, "Thrice around the circle bound, Evil sink into the ground," while you're spinning.

*(They all look at **CAT**. She doesn't move.)*

CAT. I don't believe in old superstitions.

POPPI. Fine. Fine! Give me something you're wearing and I'll do it by proxy. Maybe we can trick the theatre gods into thinking I'm really you.

> (**CAT** *pulls one of her fingerless gloves off with her teeth and hands it to* **POPPI**.)

Now everyone just stay still and for god's sake don't say that word again.

J.J. I'm so confused. What word are we talking about?

CAT. Macbe –

> (*There is a huge clap of thunder. The lights flicker on and off. Everyone is very freaked out by it except for* **J.J.** *and* **TEESHA** *who seem fascinated and entranced by it.*)

ALIX. What was that?

> (*Another louder clap of thunder. We hear some unintelligible whispers. Lights continue to flicker and the thunder rolls.*)

CHLOE. What is going on?

WILL. *(voice over) (whispered)* "Oh for a muse of fire…"

OLIVIA. Did you all hear that?

WILL. *(voice over) (whispered)* "Oh for a muse of fire…"

CAT. *(voice over)* Hermia and Lysander run away into the woods. Demetrius follows Hermia and Helena follows Demetrius.

(said 'live') Wait, that's me.

POPPI. See! I told you. This is all because of what you said.

CAT. What?

POPPI. The word. That word! You shouldn't have said it. I told you not to say it!

> (**CAT** *runs to check the doors.*)

NARRATOR *(voice over) (bewitching stage whisper)* If we shadows have offended,

Think but this, and all is mended...[8]

WILL. *(voice over)* Act 3. Scene 2...

CAT. *(voice over)* The sprites give the guys love potions to make them fall in love with the right woman, but it all ends up going wrong.

(said 'live') All the doors are locked!

OLIVIA. What?!

POPPI. I told you, it's the curse!

ALIX. Shut up!

NARRATOR *(voice over)* Think but this and all is mended...

WILL. *(voice over)* Act 3. Scene 2...

NARRATOR *(voice over)* Think but this and all is mended...

CAT. *(voice over)* Both the guys end up crazy in love with Helena, and nobody loves Hermia.

NARRATOR *(voice over)* Think but this and all is mended.

WILL. *(voice over)* Act 3 Scene 2! A clearing in the wood!

CAT & WILL & NARRATOR. *(all voice over)* NOW GO!

> *(Suddenly **J.J.** and **TEESHA** tear full throttle into the scene from Midsummer. They are fully memorized and fully committed and quite good.)*

TEESHA AS HERMIA. O me! You juggler! You canker-blossom!
You thief of love! What, have you come by night
And stole'n my love's heart from him?'

J.J. AS HELENA. Fine, i'faith!
Have you no modesty, no maiden shame,
No touch of bashfulness? What, will you tear
Impatient answers from my gentle tongue?
Fie, fie, you counterfeit! You puppet, you!

TEESHA AS HERMIA. Puppet? Why so? Ay, that way goes the game!
Now I perceive that she hath made compare
Between our statures; she hath urg'd her height;

---

[8] *Midsummer* 5.1 417

And with her personage, her tall personage,
Her height, forsooth, she hath prevail'd with him.
And are you grown so high in his esteem
Because I am so dwarfish and so low?
How low am I, thou painted maypole? Speak;
How low am I? I am not yet so low
But that my nails can reach unto thine eyes!

> *(She runs to scratch out **TEESHA/HELENA**'s eyes.)*

J.J. AS HELENA. I pray you, though you mock me, gentlemen,
Let her not hurt me. I was never curst;
I have no gift at all in shrewishness;
I am a right maid for my cowardice:
Let her not strike me. You perhaps may think,
Because she is something lower than myself,
That I can match her.

TEESHA AS HERMIA. 'Lower!' Hark, again!

J.J. AS HELENA. Good Hermia, do not be so bitter with me.
I evermore did love you, Hermia,
Did ever keep your counsels, never wrong'd you;
Save that, in love unto Demetrius,
I told him of your stealth unto this wood.
He follow'd you; for love I follow'd him.[9]

> *(We hear someone applauding from the audience and the **GIRLS** stop.)*

WILL. Well played fine ladies! Well played!

> *(A young man in Elizabethan dress comes out of the audience onto the stage applauding.)*

ALIX. Hey, how did you get in here?

WILL. My lady I know not. I was home and much consumed with writing, the sun speeding on its course toward noon. Then a cloud made shadows fall across the day. A shiver gripped my spine and did chill me to the bone.

---

[9] *Midsummer* 3.2 283

Then no light. No day. I felt my heart might overflow with icy tears. Death's cold hand could not bring a darker hour. Then did trippling voices flit about mine ears. I stood. I walked. And what figures did appear before mine eyes? Nymphs. Faeries. Oh ladies you have breathed life into these lungs this day.

POPPI. Girls? Let's get out of here.

(She runs for the doors.)

WILL. The words you spoke. Such words. Such jewels they were, as if written by God himself. What enchanted ground do I walk upon? What wood is this? What faerie land where ladies take the stage?

POPPI. How did you get in here? The doors are locked.

(J.J. and TEESHA walk up to the young man quite entranced.)

J.J. Who...? Who are you?

WILL. Oh Ladies! Will you pardon a man struck dumb by dizziness and light?

(He holds out his hand.)

Shakespeare, Will.

TEESHA. Yum.

WILL. Yes!

POPPI. *(astonished)* No.

WILL. Yes.

J.J. & TEESHA. *(confused)* What?

WILL. My name –

J.J. Will

WILL. *(finishing it)* – iam.

TEESHA. Delicious.

J.J. Delectable.

WILL. Delightful. *(beat)* I do proclaim it, with a full and honest heart, that she who stands before mine eyes this day shall forever be my queen.

J.J. & TEESHA. *(big sigh)*

POPPI. Oh my God... Oh my God! Do you know what we've done?!

CHLOE. We have hit the jackpot.

POPPI. What?

>   (**CHLOE** *runs and giddily fixes her makeup.*)

OLIVIA. Now *this?* Could get us an A.

>   (**CAT** *approaches* **WILL**, *fascinated, stares, and pokes him with a finger.*)

CAT. Wow. This is... This is... Wow...

WILL. What say you?

ALIX. Oh! Okay, I get it now. Come on Poppi. You got us, okay? I get it. Nice joke. Nice little trick to play on me, on all of us. Who is this guy anyway, some actor friend of yours from one of your outside after school activities?

WILL. What land is this?

ALIX. You can stop the acting now.

POPPI. He's not. He's – This is so cool! *(being very clear with him)* You're in Virginia.

WILL. *(confused, never having heard the word)* Virginia. Virginia? I have not heard tell of it.

POPPI. Of course you have. Wait. Wait a minute. Can I ask how old you are?

WILL. Of course dear lady. I am but eighteen years of age.

POPPI. *(a little yelp of excitement)* So, that means – Well, you were born in –

OLIVIA. 1564

ALIX. What are you doing? You're freaking me out.

POPPI. So that means, to you the year is –

WILL & OLIVIA. 1582.

POPPI. Sir Walter Raleigh didn't land here until –

POPPI & OLIVIA. 1584

POPPI. So in whatever weird reality we're existing in right now, the ground we're standing on hasn't even been discovered yet!

(**POPPI** *and* **OLIVIA** *scream and high five each other.* **KYRA** *goes and tries to get a cell phone signal with her phone. She continues this action through the following. She* **WILL** *even take* **J.J.** *and* **TEESHA***'s iPhones to try to get a signal with no luck.*)

CAT. (*poking* **WILL** *with her finger again*) Wow.

POPPI. Mr. Shakespeare. This is going to be hard to understand. But you? Are in the New World. In the colony of Virginia, which hasn't been founded yet, but it will be 'cause, well, you see, the year is –

OLIVIA. He might want to sit down for this.

POPPI. Good idea.

(**J.J.** *and* **TEESHA** *each take him by the arm and sit him down and recline at his feet.*)

Mr. Skakespeare. I know this will be hard to believe, but, through a bit of…mishandled magic –

WILL. Magic? Are you witches?

OLIVIA. I'll ignore that question and won't pop you, considering the circumstances.

POPPI. We aren't witches. But through a bit of tomfoolery, which I must – happily at the moment – take responsibility for, you have landed in the year two thousand and fifteen.

(*Several beats as he blankly stares at them.*)

CAT. Wow.

WILL. 'Tis not true.

POPPI. But it is.

OLIVIA. True, true, true.

CAT. Wow.

ALIX. I gotta sit down. Is anyone sweatin'? I'm really sweatin'.

WILL. 'Tis but a dream.

POPPI. No.

WILL. Then... The drink, the drink, how oft by night I drink.

POPPI. I'm afraid not sir. You've landed in the future.

(He stands suddenly, dramatically.)

WILL. I will not stand dumb before these monstrous words. Give proof of this!

*(Knocked to the ground by his sudden move, **J.J.** and **TEESHA** get up and move toward him. He uses his quill pen as a sword.)*

I bid you stay!

POPPI. If you'll just sit and listen –

WILL. Stay! You-you – ...Sorceress!

POPPI. We mean you no harm.

J.J. We love you!

TEESHA. 'Tis true!

OLIVIA. 'Tis what?!

WILL. Then lay it plain – this tale you tell. Where is your proof?

POPPI. Proof yes.

Ay there's the rub.[10] *(little laugh)*

(He doesn't get the joke.)

Okay then. May I ask you a few questions to help in giving you your proof?

WILL. You may. But avert your eyes lest you bewitch me further.

*(**POPPI** does.)*

All!

*(All the **GIRLS** turn away from him.)*

POPPI. Are you William Shakespeare?

WILL. Ay, this truth was but lately spoken here. Yet you did know the name before I spoke it. How this is so, I cannot say. Tis clear you did bewitch or poison me with

---

[10] *Hamlet* 3.1 65

some dram to make me speak truths aloud whilst I did sleep.

POPPI. You were born on April 23rd 1564 to Mary Arden and John Shakespeare?

> *(He moves to her, face to face, astonished and scared.)*

WILL. How do you know this?

POPPI. You are recently married.

WILL. Not yet a year.

POPPI. Her name is Anne.

> *(pause)*

WILL. *(more frightened)* Where is my wife?

POPPI. She is pregnant, isn't she?

WILL. *(terrified)* What have you done with my wife?

POPPI. It is your first child.

WILL. *(fearing the worst)* God's mercy! Where is she? What have you done with – ?

> *(He moves around the theatre frantically calling for his wife.)*

Anne…?!! Anne…?!!

POPPI. Oh! No, no, no, no, no… We haven't done anything to – She's fine… I mean, I guess she's fine –

WILL. What?! *(more frantic)* ANNE?!!!!

> *(J.J. and TEESHA follow him around trying to give comfort.)*

J.J. & TEESHA. Ooooohhhh. Will…? Come on Will… Shhh…

WILL. Stay bedazzled honey bees!

> *(They stop.)*

Where is she?

> *(No one says anything.)*

Speak! Or mark me, I will tear this building down stone by stone in search of her.

POPPI. Mr. Shakespeare please?

WILL. ANNE?!!! ANNE?!!

> *(He keeps screaming and clawing at the walls as the GIRLS try to figure out what to do.)*

J.J. Just look at him.

TEESHA. So tortured.

CHLOE. Well, is someone gonna do something 'cause this isn't going like I'd hoped.

ALIX. I'm not doing a thing. Maybe someone outside will hear his crazy ass screaming and get us out of here.

> *(KYRA is in a corner trying to remain calm. Clearly she has not been handling any of this very well and has sort of shut down, but the screaming is chipping away at her.)*

KYRA. Can someone please shut him up?

POPPI. *(to CAT)* Do something.

CAT. Why me?

> *(OLIVIA goes over and grabs WILL.)*

POPPI. 'cause you're the stage manager.

CAT. Well you're the director.

> *(He is still screaming for his wife. OLIVIA punches him in the face, flattening him to the ground. All goes quiet.)*

ALIX. Nice.

J.J. Oh no!

TEESHA. No!

> *(They run to him and try to take care of him.)*

OLIVIA. I'm – I'm sorry.

> *(She runs and hides herself in a corner.)*

WILL. What do you want of me?

POPPI. Oh nothing. Honest. Nothing at all. It's an honor just to – …I mean, yes, I have a million questions. I mean, how did you write all those plays and those –

WILL. What?

POPPI. Oh yes, of course, you don't – ...You're a writer.

WILL. 'Tis true this is my want, but what man desires will not always come to pass. Great words within my soul do shrink before they land upon the page.

POPPI. But not for long. You will become a writer. A great writer. The most famous writer the world will ever know. Your words will be so... Shrink? No. All other words, when compared to yours, will fall to dust.

> *(She goes over and picks up the complete works and brings it over and holds it out to him.)*

This. This is your life's work.

WILL. *(stunned, scared)* My life's... What?

POPPI. We study you in school. Your plays are produced all over the world in hundreds of languages.

CHLOE. And a lot of hot guys have been in your movies.

WILL. Moo – veez?

POPPI. Well, see between 1888 and 1893 Thomas Edison will –

ALIX. Oh please, can we skip the history lesson, 'cause we do not have the time?

> *(Beat.)*

POPPI. You're going to be very famous.

> *(She holds the book out to him again. He takes it.)*

WILL. Famous?

POPPI. It's all in there. Thirty seven plays.

WILL. Thirty seven?

POPPI. Yes. And they're... They're so good. You're going to write 154 Sonnets.

WILL. No.

POPPI. Yes. And there are several narrative poems. And people still argue and talk about the things you may have written but that we haven't found yet and...well, I guess since you haven't written them yet you couldn't' tell us anything about that huh?

WILL. So this is the future? And you ladies can speak words upon the stage. Women on the stage speaking lines of women.

ALIX. Yeah. We can. Imagine that.

WILL. A New World indeed.

(He caresses the book.)

I wrote…all of this? 'Tis mine?

POPPI. Yes.

WILL. I wish to read it.

POPPI. Take it. Please. It's yours.

WILL. Will you pardon me? I think it best that I retire to some private place.

POPPI. Of course.

WILL. I will not wander far.

J.J. & TEESHA. We'll be here.

*(**WILL** begins to wander off and then turns back.)*

WILL. If this were played upon a stage now, I could condemn it as an improbable fiction. [11]

(He exits.)

OLIVIA. You don't think I hurt him too bad do you?

CHLOE. Well I wouldn't count on him putting in a good word for you on his next film.

(Beat.)

CAT. What?

CHLOE. I wonder what role he'll want me to play first?

CAT. Are you high?

CHLOE. No. Just practical.

CAT. Excuse me?

CHLOE. Look, we don't even know how he got here really, and if one of you even thinks of saying that Scottish Play title thingy to see what happens or to try to get him back home or to the mother ship or whatever, I swear I will

---

[11] *Twelfth Night* 3.4 127

take you down. So it just seems logical to me that he'll be around for awhile. And even if he could go home, why would he? The plays are finished. In this century at least. Why go back to merry old – very old England and do all that work? He can just stick around here. I'll sell the story of what happened tonight to *People Magazine*, he'll make a development deal with Dreamworks, we'll buy a house in the Hollywood Hills, a beach house in Malibu, and he and I will be the power couple to end all power couples.

CAT. I think Mr. and Mrs. Macbeth might beat you out on that one.

| **CHLOE.** | **POPPI.** | **J.J. & TEESHA.** |
| Nooo!!!!! | CAT!!!!! | *(scream)* |

(When the screaming stops, they all stand still, frozen, waiting for the world to end. It doesn't.)

CHLOE. *(to CAT)* You! Have just landed on my list.

CAT. What list?

CHLOE. Oh I have a list.

CAT. Of?

CHLOE. Of people who… Who I decide need to be on the list. So when I'm famous and you try to contact me for a job or some money or an invite to a party, and I don't remember who you are, and I won't, I can check the list, and there you'll be, and I'll say, "No! No Cat. I will not help you 'cause you're on the list!"

So there.

*(**CHLOE** goes and sits and takes out a pad and pen and starts the list. The list has always been in her head, but now she has decided she needs to make an actual document.)*

ALIX. So, what do we do now?

CAT. We wait.

ALIX. Wait?

CAT. Yeah wait. We're locked in and we're not getting cell phone reception. It's really weird. I can't figure it out.

OLIVIA. Hmmm... Let's think a little bit on that one. In the last half hour, some crazy storm hit, we all started hearing voices, *(pointing at* **J.J. & TEESHA***)* these two have come down with multiple personality disorder, Chloe thinks she's a Kardashian, and oh yeah, William Shakespeare showed up! And you think it's weird we can't get a cell phone signal?!

POPPI. This is... This is like... I mean this is like a parallel universe type situation, string theory, the elegant universe, time is space, space is time, e equals m c squared – It's...! It's...! It's freaking cool.

J.J. How long do you think he'll be?

CAT. He's got a lot of plays to read.

TEESHA. I miss him already.

CHLOE. What the hell is going on with you two?

TEESHA. I can't stand it.

J.J. I need to see him now!
so tedious is this day
As is the night before some festival
To an impatient child that hath new robes
And may not wear them. [12]

(pause)

ALIX & CHLOE. What?

CAT. What did you just say?

J.J. so tedious is this day
As is the night before some festival
To an impatient child that hath new robes
And may not wear them.

POPPI. Oh my god...

OLIVIA. Why are you talking so funny?

TEESHA. Gallop apace, you fiery-footed steeds,

---

[12] *Romeo and Juliet* 3.2 28

Towards Phoebus' lodging: such a wagoner
As Phaëton would whip you to the west,
And bring in cloudy night immediately.[13]

> *(The following becomes excited chatter, almost like whispered secrets, between the **GIRLS**, willing night to come.)*

J.J. Come civil night
Thou sober suited matron all in black.[14]

TEESHA. Come gentle night, come loving black-browed night. [15]

CHLOE. What is wrong with the two of you? You're scaring me. Why are you acting like this?

> *(The sound of wind chimes or some such as **J.J.** and **TEESHA** start bringing the other **GIRLS** into their game as if casting a spell. As this continues the **GIRLS** move around the space in a bit of a haze, trying to ward off sleep.)*

J.J. Tis now the very witching time of night.[16]

CHLOE. Stop it. You're making me feel funny.

TEESHA. Now the hungry lion roars,
And the wolf behowls the moon;[17]

POPPI. I'm tired. Are any of you tired?

J.J. Now it is the time of night.[18]

ALIX. Shhh…please… I need to sleep.

TEESHA. Now it is the time of night…

KYRA. To sleep perchance to dream…[19]

> *(The **GIRLS** are deathly tired but their feet keep them wandering. Whispers are heard, maybe*

---

[13] *Romeo and Juliet* 3.2 1
[14] *Romeo and Juliet* 3.2 10
[15] *Romeo and Juliet* 3.2 20
[16] *Hamlet* 3.2 380
[17] *Midsummer* 5.1 365
[18] *Midsummer* 5.1 373
[19] *Hamlet* 3.1 65

> *music, wind in the trees…sounds of night…then a voice…)*

NARRATOR *(voice over) (gently)* I know a bank where the wild thyme blows,

> *(As she continues the **GIRLS** begin to echo her almost in a trance. Note the overlap should start where the / is.)*

I know a bank/ where the wild thyme blows,

GIRLS. I know a bank where the wild thyme blows,

NARRATOR *(voice over)* Where oxlips /and the nodding violet grows,

GIRLS. Where oxlips and the nodding violet grows,

NARRATOR *(voice over)* Quite over-canopied /with luscious woodbine,

GIRLS. Quite over-canopied with luscious woodbine,

NARRATOR *(voice over)* With sweet musk-roses /and with eglantine:

GIRLS. With sweet musk-roses and with eglantine:

NARRATOR *(voice over)* There sleep (young ladies)/ sometime of the night,

GIRLS. There sleep (young ladies) sometime of the night,

NARRATOR *(voice over)* **& GIRLS.** Lull'd in these flowers with dances and delight;[20]

> *(The **GIRLS** are asleep.)*

(voice over) Sleep dwell upon thine eyes, peace in they breast

Would I were sleep and peace so sweet to rest.[21]

> *(**WILL** wanders back into the space. He looks rumpled, undone, as if he hasn't slept in days and days, and yet he is very much aglow. He carries* The Complete Works *and is reading from the end of* The Tempest.*)*

---

[20] *Midsummer* 2.1 249
[21] *Romeo and Juliet* 2.3 186

WILL. Now my charms are all o'erthrown,
And what strength I have's mine own,
Which is most faint: now, 'Tis true,
I must be here confined by you....[22]

> *(He notices the **GIRLS** asleep and wanders amongst them. His focus goes back to the book and reads.)*

But release me from my bands
With the help of your good hands:
Gentle breath of yours my sails
Must fill, or else my project fails,
Which was to please. Now I want
Spirits to enforce, art to enchant...[23]

> *(He closes the book.)*

T'have seen what I have seen, see what I see...[24]
And now I know all that I will know.

(with sudden buoyant cocky energy) I'm good. I'm really, really bloody good!!

> *(He rouses the **GIRLS**.)*

Ladies?!! Awake! Arise!!!

> *(They all stir, mumble and grumble.)*

CHLOE. What's going on?

> *(**KYRA** awakens and crossing the room comes face to face with **WILL**. He stops her.)*

WILL. Your face is a book, where men may read strange matters.[25]

KYRA. Excuse me?

WILL. There is occasions and causes why and wherefore in all things.[26]

---

[22] *Tempest* Epilogue 1
[23] *Tempest* Epilogue 9
[24] *Hamlet* 3.1 162
[25] *Macbeth* 1.5 62
[26] *Henry V* 5.1 3

> (**J.J.** *and* **TEESHA** *suddenly realize he is back.*)

J.J. & TEESHA. *(scream)*
CAT. Whoa.
ALIX. Really?
WILL. So tell me ladies, which of my masterpieces is your favorite?

> *(The following is at break neck speed.)*

J.J. Well for me –
TEESHA. It's so hard to choose –
J.J. Impossible to pick –
TEESHA. Which best is best –
J.J. Which great is greatest –
TEESHA. Do you like Comedy or Tragedy?
J.J. History or Romance?
TEESHA. And the problem plays –
J.J. The problem plays?
BOTH. Not a problem for me.
J.J. I mean pick a king.
TEESHA. Any king.
J.J. Choose?
TEESHA. How can you choose?
J.J. *King John*
TEESHA. *King Lear*
J.J. *King Richard the Second.*
TEESHA. *King Richard the Third*
J.J. And all those Henry's
TEESHA. So many Henry's
J.J. *Henry the Fourth*
TEESHA. Part One or Two?
J.J. *Henry the Sixth*
TEESHA. One two or three.
BOTH. And oh for a muse of fire!
> *King Henry the Fifth*!

WILL. Oh Ladies!

ALIX. Oh brother.

WILL. Oh my. Do you not share your classmates' passion for my work?

ALIX. No. No I don't.

POPPI. Alix, don't do this.

WILL. You have some quarrel with my plays?

ALIX. Yeah I do. That list they just spouted of all those kings, fighting for thrones, killing off their family members for a crown. That doesn't have anything to do with me. You don't have any idea what I have to fight for and what I'm gonna have to keep fighting for. I got my own history to make, so you can keep yours to yourself.

WILL. You seek a battle of thine own. Show me then. *(holding out the book)* Read *King Henry the Fifth* speaking to his troops before the battle at Agincourt. They are out numbered. They are sure to die. But he – the King – must rouse his troops to victory. Show what your heart be made of!

(He hands her the book. She reads but not with much passion.)

ALIX. he which hath no stomach to this fight,
Let him depart; his passport shall be made,
And crowns for convoy put into his purse;
We would not die in that man's company
That fears his fellowship to die with us.

WILL. What do those words mean?

ALIX. I guess something like if any of the guys there are too scared to fight then they can leave and the rest will be so happy to have him go that they'll give him money to get out of there cause they don't want anything to do with such a coward.

WILL. Go on.

ALIX. This day is called the feast of Cris – Cris – I can't do it. It's stupid.

*(**WILL** takes over the speech not needing the script.)*

WILL. This day is called the feast of Crispian.[ii]
He that shall see this day, and live old age,
Will yearly on the vigil feast his neighbours,
And say 'To-morrow is Saint Crispian.'
Then will he strip his sleeve and show his scars,
And say 'These wounds I had on Crispin's day.

You also wish to lead an army toward whatever cause you see fit. Even faced with ten thousand warring enemies you will stand strong, and you will change the world! Now read!

*(**ALIX** takes the book and reads with passion and fervor.)*

ALIX. This story shall the good man teach his son;
And Crispin Crispian shall ne'er go by,
From this day to the ending of the world,
But we in it shall be remembered –
We few, we happy few, we band of brothers.
For he today that sheds his blood with me
Shall be my brother; be he ne'er so vile,
This day shall gentle his condition;
And gentlemen in England now abed
Shall think themselves accurs'd they were not here,
And hold their manhoods cheap whiles any speaks
That fought with us upon Saint Crispin's day! [27]

*(**WILL** and the other **GIRLS** (except for **KYRA**) cheer.)*

KYRA. So is *everyone* who doesn't fight a coward?

WILL. My lady?

KYRA. You make war all cheering and shouting and glory. What happens then to someone who doesn't leave, who does stay to fight, but when it comes right down to it and he has to pull the trigger, he can't because

---
[27] *Henry V* 4.3 35

to take another life just isn't part of how he – of how my brother saw the world, so he died refusing to fight. Is he a coward to you? Is he...can I still call him my brother?

(He goes to her.)

WILL. Yes, oh yes.

Praising what is lost
Makes the remembrance dear. [28]

(Something breaks, releases in her. She can finally cry.)

Will you read this?

(He hands her the book.)

From *Julius Caesar*.

(She reads to where he points in the book.)

KYRA. His life was gentle; and the elements
So mixed in him, that Nature might stand up,
And say to all the world, this was a man. [29]

(She closes the book gently.)

Thank you.

*(**POPPI** moves to **KYRA** and takes her hand. **KYRA** lays her head in **POPPI**'s lap as **CHLOE** approaches **WILL**.)*

CHLOE. Mr. Shakespeare? Will. I just have to tell you: Thank you.

WILL. For?

CHLOE. For Juliet. For Ophelia. For Viola and all those other beautiful, untouchable, perfect, women that you created. You've made me possible.

WILL. Pardon?

CHLOE. Well, I'm the ideal right? I'm what you told men they should want.

---

[28] *All's Well That Ends Well* 5.3 19
[29] *Julius Caesar* 5.5 73

WILL. Oh no., no, no, 'Tis not what I meant –

CHLOE. Let me be your Juliet. Can I read it for you?

J.J. No I want to be Juliet

TEESHA. No I do!

CHLOE. You two stay out of this! I'm the one clearly!

J.J. Yeah right?!

TEESHA. Both of you out of the way, it's mine!

WILL. Good ladies, please!

CHLOE. You choose then!

J.J. Yeah, you pick.

TEESHA. Which one of us is your Juliet?

CHLOE. Come on, do it, pick someone.

(He steps back to get a better look.)

WILL. I choose…

(The three wait with breathless anticipation.)

You.

*(He points to **OLIVIA**.)*

OLIVIA. Me?

CHLOE & J.J. & TEESHA. Her?

WILL. Ay, you will be my Juliet. Do you know the play?

OLIVIA. Yeah. We study it in class. But that's not me.

WILL. 'Twas written 400 years ago, but I have never heard it read aloud.

OLIVIA. I – I cant.

WILL. Please? I will not toy with you.

(He hands her the book. She takes it and reads tentatively.)

OLIVIA AS JULIET. Oh Romeo, Romeo
Wherefore art thou Romeo?
Deny thy father and refuse thy name.
Or if thou wilt not, be but sworn my love
And I'll no longer be a Capulet.

WILL AS ROMEO. She speaks.

> O speak again bright angel, for thou art
> As glorious to this night –

OLIVIA. *(closing the book)* Stop it! Now you're just making fun.

WILL. No!

OLIVIA. I'm not a glorious *bright* angel.

WILL. Oh but you are.

> *(He picks up the book and starts leafing through it.)*

Will you recite some other words for me?

OLIVIA. No.

WILL. This is Sonnet 130.

> My mistress' eyes are nothing like the sun;
> Coral is far more red than her lips' red;
> If snow be white, why then her breasts are dun;
> If hairs be wires, black wires grow on her head.
> I have seen roses damasked, red and white,
> But no such roses see I in her cheeks;
> And in some perfumes is there more delight
> Than in the breath that from my mistress reeks.
> I love to hear her speak, yet well I know
> That music hath a far more pleasing sound;
> I grant I never saw a goddess go;
> My mistress when she walks treads on the ground.

Wilt thou read just the last two lines for me?

> *(He points to the text. She reads.)*

OLIVIA. And yet, by heaven, I think my love as rare
As any she belied with false compare. [30]

WILL. I wrote of Juliet yes, but when I wrote this sonnet, something had quite changed in me.

OLIVIA. I guess.

---

[30] Sonnet 130

WILL. What kind of woman do I want with this sonnet?

OLIVIA. I don't know.

WILL. You do.

OLIVIA. Someone – someone not so…not so perfect. Someone like me?

WILL. Yes. Not some unreachable figure whom I shall only know through longing, but one who stands here next to me. Who is all there is.

ANNE. *(from offstage screaming)* WILL SHAKESPEARE?!!!!

WILL. And lo where she comes!

> *(**WILL**'s wife **ANNE HATHAWAY** enters, eight months pregnant.)*

ANNE. Where hast thou been?! I have spent the day and lose count of the hours past nightfall calling out your name. "Will…?! WILL SHAKESPEARE?!!" Dogs did howl. Cats pricked up their ears unable to ignore. Our good neighbors shut their doors in need of rest. All of Stratford now knows thy name having heard it bellowed up and down and twice 'round the world in hopes of reaching you. I have not slept one wink. And where art thou? Unkempt amongst these…ladies, the sole patron of this good and filthy brothel!

OLIVIA. Brothel?! Did you say brothel?! *(under her breath to **CAT**)* Quick, what's a brothel?

CAT. A whorehouse.

OLIVIA. That's what I thought. *(back to **ANNE**)* A BROTHEL?!!

ANNE. You did hear me, my fine young lady.

WILL. Good Anne –

ANNE. Come not within the measure of my wrath!

WILL. Go to, charm your tongue.

ANNE. I will not charm my tongue.[31]

WILL. My dearest wife, thou hast figured this puzzle wrong. Through some playfulness of God himself, we have

---

[31] *Othello* 5.2 181

fallen into the future. These fine ladies are students in a school some four hundred years past when we did walk the earth.

ANNE. What sayest thou?

WILL. 'Tis true. 'Tis strange and wondrous true.

> *(ANNE is shocked and stunned. She looks around trying to take it in, then just accepts the circumstances and rips back into WILL.)*

ANNE. Hast thou grown weary of the Stratford ladies thou hast known? I figured the good ladies of London would be next to taste thy charms. Nay, 'tis too base and common for my proud, arrogant Will. Still, I did not think thou wouldst turn to sorcery to flee your cold, married bed. Be careful my fair ladies, my Will can bewitch and charm a fish to curse the sea.

J.J. Oh he's not a sorcerer!

TEESHA. He's divine!

ANNE. *(laughing)* They take thee for a God? I warn you ladies, the devil hath power to assume a pleasing shape.

J.J. You take that back!

ANNE. When he is best, he is a little worse than a man; and when he is worst, he is little better than a beast.[32]

TEESHA. Ok, now you're gonna get it!

> *(TEESHA and J.J. lunge for ANNE to rip her eyes out. The other GIRLS try to keep them from ANNE.)*

J.J. Your husband is a great man!

WILL. 'Tis true my love. It is indeed the future, and I do become a writer, just as it is foretold within my dreams.

> *(He holds out the book to her.)*

They study me Anne. In schools. I write plays and sonnets and they are spoken across the world in every tongue. I am known more than even I could imagine I would be known. They say I will be the greatest writer who has ever walked the earth.

---

[32] *Merchant* 1.2

*(Pause. As **WILL** puts the book in **ANNE**'s hands. Then **ANNE** begins to laugh – a big hearty – crushing laugh as she shakes the book, sending page after page fluttering to the floor.)*

ANNE. Thou a writer? Thou famous? Time travel doth dull the brain, perhaps? Cause one to see the day for night and night as if 'twere day? Makes young girls think a boy be a man, a nothing be a god. Enough of thy stories, my good husband. Enough of thy dreams and strange fantasies. Let us find our way to home, and please, I beg of thee, Will, no more talk of plays and –

WILL. WILLIAM!!

(beat)

I?! Am William Shakespeare.

(He buttons up his doublet, suddenly needing and wanting to look the part. He goes to his wife and practically hisses/whispers in her ear.)

And who art thou?

*(He turns to the **GIRLS** to say goodbye.)*

Ladies? I give you my most humble thanks.
I wish you well and so I take my leave,
And pray you know me if we meet again.[33]

*(He leaves. There is a long silence. **ANNE** cannot move. The **GIRLS** are unsure of what to say or do. **ANNE** suddenly remembers she is not alone.)*

ANNE. Forgive this mess I pray you.

*(She gets to her knees to pick up the scattered pages. **CHLOE** and **OLIVIA** try to help.)*

CHLOE. Please, let us –

OLIVIA. Yes, let us help.

ANNE. No 'tis mine to remedy.

---

[33] *Merchant* 4.1 417

*(The **GIRLS** back off. **ANNE** picks up page after page, looking at them with wonder. She stops on one and reads aloud:)*

If music be the food of love, play on.[34]

Do you know these words?

CAT. Ummm... Yes Ma'am.

ANNE. From what play do they spring?

CAT. *Twelfth Night*, Ma'am.

*(**ANNE** picks up another page and reads.)*

ANNE. All the world's a stage,
And all the men and women merely players:[35]
And those words?

KYRA. I think... Are they from *As You Like It*?

ANNE. 'Tis true.

KYRA. We read it in class.

*(**ANNE** gathers up more pages looking at them with wonder. She stops on another particular page and reads.)*

ANNE. Let me not to the marriage of true minds
Admit impediments. Love is not love
Which alters when it alteration finds,

POPPI & ANNE. Or bends with the remover to remove:

POPPI. O no. It is an ever-fixed mark
That looks on tempests and is never shaken;
Sonnet 116. It's my favorite.

*(**ANNE** picks up another page and reads.)*

ANNE. To be, or not to be –

ALL THE GIRLS. – that is the question:

(beat)

POPPI. It's a very famous speech.

---

[34] *Twelfth Night* 1.1 1
[35] *As You Like It* 2.7 139

CHLOE. And Mel Gibson and Kenneth Branagh and Ethan Hawke have all made movies of it.

(pause)

ANNE. So he will be all that he did proclaim himself to be?

(They just look at her. Maybe one or two shake their heads yes.)

And what of me are you taught?

(No one can respond.)

Is there nothing?

CAT. Not much is said.

*(**ANNE** continues to pick up pages more frantically gathering them in her arms. **POPPI** tries to make it better.)*

POPPI. But – ... But that's only because not much is known about you 'cause you didn't do anything really except to marry him so – *(a sudden stop realizing what she has said)*

*(**ANNE** stops like she's been punched in the gut.)*

ANNE. Such is the life I will return to. Do not think me a fool. I have always known his wish to be remembered past this little time we walk upon the earth. My fault is thinking it was nothing more than fancy. *(looking at the pages in her arms)* Fancy. Such...trifles bound themselves to madness in mine eyes. What does one gain from being remembered? Even now, after this night, I do not need to be remembered. But I did not foresee my long life spent knowing I shall be forgot.

(She notices the pages she now holds clasped to her chest.)

I fear this is to be the last time I shall hold my husband in mine arms.

(She glances down and sees some words on one particular page. She reads them aloud.)

Tomorrow, and tomorrow, and tomorrow,

Creeps in this petty pace from day-to-day,
To the last syllable of recorded time;
And all our yesterdays have lighted fools
The way to dusty death. Out, out, brief candle!
Life's but a walking shadow, a poor player,
That struts and frets his hour upon the stage,
And then is heard no more… [36]

> *(She lets the pages fall from her arms and scatter about the floor and then begins to exit.)*

J.J. No, no, please, you must take them.
TEESHA. How will he know what to write?
ANNE. 'Tis written in the stars.

> *(She wanders off. The* **GIRLS** *stand silent and still for a long moment. Then* **KYRA**'s *phone starts ringing. She doesn't move for it.* **TEESHA**'s *starts ringing, then* **J.J.**'s. *Each of the* **GIRLS** *phone starts ringing. They all move and pick up their phones and turn them off. Silence. They gather their things.)*

CHLOE. See you guys tomorrow in class?
OLIVIA. Anyone want to grab some food or something?
POPPI. Naw. Gotta start that twenty five page paper.

> *(The* **GIRLS** *aren't quite sure what to do. Is this it? Was this just a singular night? The* **GIRLS** *start to exit. Suddenly* **CAT** *drops her backpack and moves to the center of the room and holds both of her hands out to her side.)*

CAT. Double, double toil and trouble;
   Fire burn, and cauldron bubble.

> *(***OLIVIA** *drops her backpack and goes and takes* **CAT**'s *hand.)*

OLIVIA. Double, double toil and trouble;

---

[36] *Macbeth* 5.5 19

Fire burn, and cauldron bubble.

> (**CHLOE** *drops her purse and goes and takes* **OLIVIA**'s *hand.* **TEESHA** *goes to the circle and joins. Then* **KYRA**, *then* **J.J.**, *and then* **ALIX**. **POPPI** *stands still, moved by her classmates' actions, and she drops her backpack and goes to finish the circle.*)

CAT. When shall we all meet again,
In thunder, lightning, or in rain?

ALL THE OTHER GIRLS. When shall we meet again,
In thunder, lightning, or in rain?

CAT. When the hurlyburly's done,
When the battle's lost and won.

ALL THE OTHER GIRLS. When the hurlyburly's done,
When the battle's lost and won.

CAT. That will be ere the set of sun.

ALL THE OTHER GIRLS. That will be ere the set of sun.

CAT. Where shall we meet?

ALL THE OTHER GIRLS. Upon the heath!

CAT. There to meet Mac –!

ALL THE OTHER GIRLS. SHHHHH!

(blackout)

End of Play